VILLAGERS

VILLAGERS

Athabaskan Indian Life
Along the Yukon River

CLAIRE FEJES

Random House
New York

Library of Congress Cataloging in Publication Data

Fejes, Claire.
Villagers, Athabaskan Indian life along the Yukon
River.

Bibliography: p.
1. Athapascan Indians—Social conditions.
I. Title. II. Title: Athabaskan Indian life along the
Yukon River.
E99.A86F44   970.004'97   80–6039
ISBN 0–394–51673–7   AACR2

Manufactured in the United States of America

9 8 7 6 5 4 3 2

FIRST EDITION

Acknowledgments

This book is dedicated to the people of the Yukon and Tanana rivers who showed me such warm hospitality, to their wise elders and to those children yet unborn. I am indebted to Chief and Mrs. Peter John and the people of Minto; Chief and Mrs. Andrew Isaac; Charlotte Adams; Mary Tall Mountain; Dr. Wallace Olsen, professor of anthropology; Paul McCarthy, archivist; David Hales of the University of Alaska Library; Marvin Smith and his staff at the Noel Wien Memorial Library; and Captain and Mrs. Art Peterson.

With gratitude and love to my husband, Joe, and to my many friends who gave me their support. While this book is no substitute for the in-depth work Indians will be producing about their own lives, it is my hope that the people will find this account harmonious with their own knowledge, feelings and love of the land.

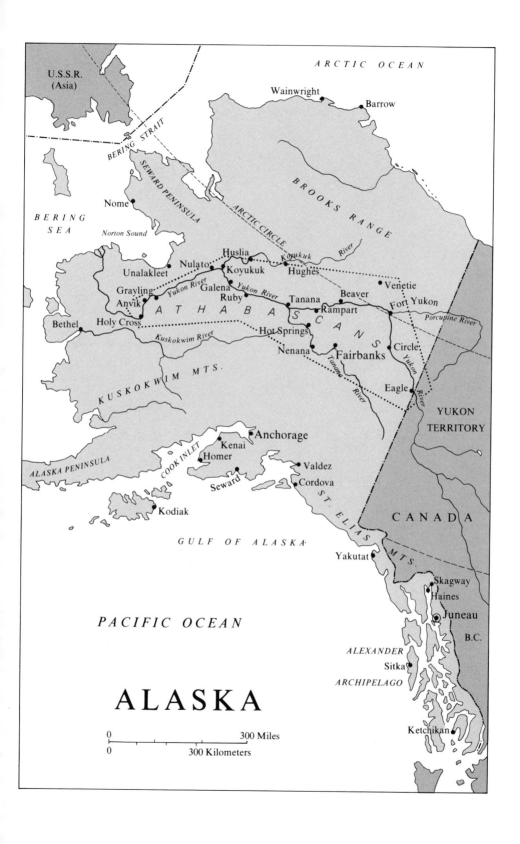

ARCTIC OCEAN

U.S.S.R.
(Asia)

Wainwright   Barrow

BERING STRAIT

BROOKS RANGE

SEWARD PENINSULA

Nome

BERING
SEA

Norton Sound

ARCTIC CIRCLE

Koyukuk   River

Huslia
Nulato   Koyukuk   Hughes
Unalakleet
Galena   Venetie
Grayling   Yukon River   Beaver
Anvik   Ruby   Yukon River   Tanana   Fort Yukon
A T H A B A S C A N S   Rampart   Porcupine River
Bethel   Holy Cross
Kuskokwim River   Hot Springs   Circle
Nenana   Fairbanks
Yukon River

KUSKOKWIM MTS.

Tanana River

Eagle

YUKON
TERRITORY

Anchorage
Kenai
Homer
ALASKA PENINSULA   COOK INLET   Seward   Valdez
Cordova
ST. ELIAS MTS.   CANADA

Kodiak

GULF OF ALASKA

Yakutat

PACIFIC OCEAN

Skagway
Haines
Juneau
B.C.

ALEXANDER
Sitka
ARCHIPELAGO

ALASKA

Ketchikan

0   300 Miles
0   300 Kilometers

Contents

PART I

CHAPTER 1
Beginnings   *3*

CHAPTER 2
Old Minto Remembered   *9*

CHAPTER 3
New Minto   *14*

CHAPTER 4
Chief Peter John of Minto   *24*

CHAPTER 5
On the Tanana River   *33*

CHAPTER 6
The Yukon   *40*

CHAPTER 7
Nuchalawoya   *47*

CHAPTER 8
Galena   *57*

CHAPTER 9
Ella Vernetti of Koyukuk   *64*

CHAPTER 10
Nulato   *69*

CHAPTER 11
   Kaltag   *82*
CHAPTER 12
   Grayling   *90*
CHAPTER 13
   Anvik   *97*
CHAPTER 14
   Holy Cross   *105*

PART II
CHAPTER 15
   Nenana   *123*
CHAPTER 16
   Rampart   *129*
CHAPTER 17
   Beaver Remembered   *134*
CHAPTER 18
   Beaver Revisited   *151*
CHAPTER 19
   Fort Yukon   *156*
CHAPTER 20
   Circle City   *168*
CHAPTER 21
   Eagle   *171*
CHAPTER 22
   Potlatch   *184*

   Bibliography   *199*

PART 1

CHAPTER 1

Beginnings

Eldest Kinswoman
You cry to me through smoke
*   of tribal fires.*
I echo the primal voice—
The drumming blood . . .

Walk beside me. Feel
How these winds move, the way
These mornings breathe.
Let me see you new
In this light.

MARY TALL MOUNTAIN,
from "The Figure in Clay"

Iᴛ is January in Fairbanks, Alaska.
The temperature is fifty-eight degrees below zero. Icicles hang threat-
eningly from our log cabin, some of them four feet long. A thick rim
of frost crystallizes along the bottom edge of our kitchen door. Ice fog
has settled thickly; I cannot see across the street. Near my window, tree
limbs are encased in ice. At three-thirty in the afternoon it is dark as
night in the Tanana Valley where we live.

A raven perched on the top of the spruce tree disturbs the stillness
with his cacophony. With his glistening blackness and huge wingspan,

he appears as a reincarnation of that other raven of ancient Indian lore, the creator of all life.

I think of the first people to live along the banks of the Tanana River. How could they subsist in their tentlike shelters of moose and caribou hides? How could they travel on a day such as this through deep snow to hunt for scarce game? How could the women keep their babies warm? I marvel at their ability to cut wood with stone adzes and fashion snowshoes with flint knives.

Winters in Alaska are long and bitter, among the most severe in the world. Athabaskan Indians survive in a hostile subarctic environment. They have adapted to a cold, harsh life where darkness prevails most of the snowy winter and mosquitoes plague the summer.

In anthropology courses at universities, it seems that Indians are important only for their hunting habits, skull measurements and languages. I wanted to know them as people. I had read all the books I could about Athabaskan Indians, spoken with anthropologists and linguists, and learned that the Indians had never written an account of their own history. They had no written language, only an oral tradition. All the books I read were by authors who were interested in various aspects of Indian life—exploration, mining, artifacts, language, religion. Books by traders betrayed their main concern: making a profit on furs. Rarely did anyone write from the Indians' point of view.

For many years, with my sleeping bag and paint box, I had visited isolated Eskimo and Indian villages from our home in Fairbanks, painting the life of the people in the Arctic. Surely there is a universal language of the heart, for we were able to communicate through facial expressions and body language rather than solely through words. I wanted to portray the essence of Indian life as I felt it, as my eyes saw it and as my hands guiding my paintbrush expressed it. All my life I have been first an artist, interpreting life in visual terms. It is only after I have finished a painting and I am overwhelmed by impressions that words come.

Most of the Indian villages I had visited had populations of 150 to 250, and in each everyone seemed related to everyone else. Many people often shared one cabin: relatives, immediate family, friends and always shy or noisy children. Soft-spoken mothers could be seen bent over the sewing or washbasins or throwing chunks of wood into fires. Old grandmothers sat near Yukon stoves, hands busy with tasks, cooking what had been hunted.

These people welcomed me and shared their food with me. Yet there was much that remained unspoken between us; they were strangers to me and I to them. They must have wondered how I had the freedom to travel and work as an artist. I marveled at their toughness, their ability to adapt to their harsh environment.

The passage of the Alaska Native Claims Settlement Act on December 18, 1971, awarded 40 million acres of land and $962.5 million to Native village and regional corporations in Alaska. In the last few years Natives have become more purposeful in their demands for a better life. They are becoming more militant, aware of their power and economic clout, seeking their own roots and heritage. The bush vote is now recognized in politics as a powerful force. To understand and record the heritage of the Athabaskans and changes in their life styles resulting from the Native claims settlement, I decided to visit Athabaskan villages along the Tanana and Yukon rivers, where once the Indians traveled as nomads.

For years I had asked the Petersons, who owned the Yutana Barge Line in Nenana, to let me know if they ever had space aboard. The barge stopped at Indian villages along the Tanana and Yukon rivers, delivering supplies. I was delighted when Adriana, Captain Art Peterson's wife, invited me to accompany them on the last trip of 1974.

The tree limbs at home were weighted down with ripe chokecherries. Cranberries and blueberries were ripe in the woods and tundra. I would leave without picking them.

As I watched a raven from the window, I stuffed a rucksack full of warm clothing, including a Cowichan Indian sweater and a sleeping bag. My oil box and other paint supplies were already packed for the boat trip.

Our voyage would take us from Nenana to the village of Tanana, then down the Yukon River to Holy Cross. There are about 10,000 Athabaskans living in 37 percent of Alaskan territory and throughout the western half of Canada. Their neighbors are Eskimos. The Athabaksans we would visit speak six dialects: Kutchin, Ingalik, Han, Koyukon, Tanana and Holikachuk. The name they call themselves is a variation of the word *Dené*, the People. Other Indians of the same language family are found in Washington, Oregon and California, and also in the southwestern part of the United States, where they are known as Apaches and Navajos.

On August 15, 1974, my husband, Joe, drove me to Nenana, the headquarters of the barge line. Then he flew with the Arctic Chamber Orchestra to Sitka, thence to other Native villages where he would be performing as a violinist. The orchestra played for people who had never seen a violin or many of the other musical instruments before, and who were hearing Beethoven and Bach for the first time in their lives.

The boat had three decks. Big gold letters painted on one side proclaimed her *The Yukon*. Adriana's father, Captain Black, used to freight goods down the Yukon in a sixty-five footer called *The Pelican*. "He used to cut wood all winter to make money for the next trip," she recalled. "Now the Alaska Railroad owns this boat, and we lease it from them."

The lowest deck held the cook's quarters, the galley and dining rooms, and the various cabins for the crew. The top deck held the wheelhouse, where the captain and pilot presided. My tiny room, on the middle deck over the engines, was painted battleship gray and had a single bunk and bulb, small window, sink, table, chair and closet. The Petersons never took paying passengers on their freighting barge, so I felt lucky to be aboard as a friend of Adriana's.

Walking around the deck, I smelled fresh coffee brewing in the galley. Everything aboard clamored, rattled, chugged, grunted or whistled. *The Yukon* had two 600-hp diesel engines with twin screws. It pushed a barge loaded with a thousand tons of freight.

In the wheelhouse Captain Art Peterson sat in his swivel chair, which Adriana called his "ulcer seat." He was a big man with a crew-cut and a pleasant craggy face. He walked loosely, hands in his pockets, laughing easily. "Welcome aboard," he shouted as he waved.

The landscape was an orgy of autumnal arctic colors. The

magenta flowers of the fireweed sprouted tall tufts of white fluffy seeds; the rose hips were full of yellow meat, and the cranberry clusters were about to fall off the vines. Yellowjackets guarded their territories, and the earth was wet and spongy on the trails around Nenana.

Ahead of us, sandy beaches were heaped with driftwood; tree snags bent over the Tanana. The river reflected the golden birches, flaming against the tall green-black spruce spires. The main channel of the Tanana River was wide, about seven hundred feet across, with channels of slow-shifting sand and gravel islands going off in every direction. The deepest water along the rivers was often near the banks, and that was where "sweepers," trees that hung over the edge, were found. The boat swerved from one side of the river to the other to avoid hitting them.

An island of tall tamaracks disappeared around the bend when I tried to sketch it, becoming flat country, thick with willows and stringy spruce. Ground cover was a rich tapestry in fern, bramble and moss, wild pink roses and berries.

As we chugged along there were no signs of birds, ducks, animals or humans. Not a single shed or house, only rolling clouds in a pale, washed-out sky. The river seemed a milky swirl, as in a Chinese scroll painting.

The Fathometer on *The Yukon* read five feet as we crawled along. It would be hours before we would pass Minto, an Indian village. Adriana noted that the channel had changed: "There is a low waterline and sand bars that are not usually visible."

"A small calf and cow moose sat on that sand bar last trip," Captain Art pointed out. We slowly drifted by fields of bromegrass in a clearing—a good moose pasture.

"Sweepers all around the bend, a tight squeeze," said the captain, steering carefully. "Saw a flock of geese feeding here last trip." Cottonwoods and birches hung over the river's edge.

Agnes, the cook, popped her head out of the hatch to report, "Dinner's ready." We all went down to eat a fattening meal of baked ham, sweet potatoes and cherry cobbler.

I spent the evening trying to sketch. Two mallards and a black crow spotted the landscape, and a lone sea gull flew neatly down the center of the channel and landed on driftwood. I took a deep breath, full of excitement for what lay ahead.

CHAPTER 2

Old Minto Remembered

The earth was small at first, and the land gradually increased. There was a small band of people going about here and there in the grass. They warmed themselves in the grass, and grew with the earth. They slept, and found food placed near them, which they ate. Clothes were provided in the same way, and also berries. At length they met a man, who spoke to them angrily, and asked them why they had taken his food and berries. "For this you will obey my commands." The man went away—they did not know where—but he reappeared to them from time to time. His village was across the slough from Nĭhltĕ' ûxaidlĭ' ñktû, where he lived with other men, but no women. Going about in his canoe, he heard the noise of talking women. He went up quietly and launched his spear, which passed through the parka of one of them. The rest turned into geese and flew away; but he captured this one and took her home. The rest of the men began to get wives in the same way. They gave their children food and clothes as they grew up, taught them different tongues, and sent them away, up and down the river, which they peopled.

JOHN W. CHAPMAN,
"Athabaskan Traditions from the
Lower Yukon," Journal of American Folklore,
vol. 16, 1903

THE boat pushing the freight barge passed the gaping doors of the Old Minto village with its deserted cabins and caches. No smoke came out of the chimneys. The houses were going to ruin, inhabited only by field mice and squirrels, which scurried through the cracked windows. The village looked as if the people had left in a hurry: clothes were strewn, washing machines, bicycle parts, cans were discarded—all detritus from a people salvaging what they could before the flood hit. A chest of drawers spilled its contents across the silt-laden floor, exuding a feeling of urgency. "Jesus Saves" was painted in big letters on a roof.

Three Indians in army parkas rested on banks near a motorboat at an old fish camp. The sun shone on red-orange salmon hanging on their rack; and I saw ravens on the vast inlet cove, their glossy wings gaining altitude in lifting spirals. Captain Art steered the boat, sweating out the turn, missing the bank by a few feet, avoiding the huge sweepers jutting out.

In the fall of 1967, I had visited Minto for the first time. Then the people were still living near the Tanana River in their log cabins, their racks full of drying salmon. Two weeks after my visit, the rampaging Tanana had flooded the village, an almost annual occurrence. The Tanana and Yukon villages were also flooded, and the Chena River, a tributary of the Tanana that flows through Fairbanks, rose dangerously, causing Fairbanks as well as the river villages to be declared disaster areas. The river, lifeline and provider, had become an enemy. The inhabitants of Minto decided to move near the Tolovana River, where foothills would secure them from further floods, but in so doing they changed their traditional way of life.

I had traveled to Minto with Fabian Carey, a trapper friend who piloted a small Cessna. Old Minto was nestled against the muddy river with its steep banks and thick willow bushes. Tangled rose hips had twined around the vetches, wild irises grew among the white flowers, and trails led everywhere through the thorny wild-rose bushes. Canada geese, pintail, mallard, teal and widgeon nested there, and in the bogs were grouse, ptarmigan and spruce hen. Along the banks swam beaver and muskrat. The rivers abounded with whitefish, pike and salmon, and in the hills were bear, fox, wolf, mink, weasel, lynx, squirrel and rabbit.

The heat had been intense, and the scent of fish had emanated from the small one-room log cabins. Often under one roof, washing, sewing, toolmaking, thawing and cooking of game took place. Most cabins had a small pit under the floor, which was used as a root cellar. Ten people could live in each cabin, with new life being born and old people dying in it in an ever-changing chain.

One pump at the center of the village had supplied water, which was hauled two bucketfuls at a time. In addition, the people had relied on the river, snow and rainwater.

There had been only a few salaried jobs in Minto, including school janitor, store manager and mail carrier. Most of the men had had to work away from home to support their families.

Once the entire village had worked for three months cutting sixteen hundred cords of wood, selling it to the steamboats to earn money to open a store: everyone had cut his share of peeled logs and paid a poll tax of two muskrat pelts. The store was now deserted. Flies hummed among the few canned stuff.

On top of the store counter had been some birch-bark baskets. An old wrinkled woman, her skin brown as the darkest shade of birch, had sat outdoors making a baby basket. Worn hands held the bark that she had laboriously peeled off the tree. She used blueberries and red ocher to dye the spruce-root binding, and sewed trade beads or animal claws along the back as rattles. She had tied her own babies into such cradles with babiche thongs. "Our babies rest their backs against part of a tree," she explained. Her mother had used moss or squirrels' nests for diapers.

The women used to make birch baskets for cooking and storing food. They cooked meat by heating stones red hot, then dropping them in the baskets until the meat was done. Sometimes they roasted meat over a fire or froze it, eating it raw, dried or smoked. To keep food in the summer, they dug holes in the ground down to permafrost, which served as natural iceboxes. Women burned Buhach, a mosquito repellent, in order to work outdoors.

"I raised ten kids by washboard. No Pampers," the old woman told me, pulling a strand of her gray hair back. Even in the winter, because of the low humidity, she hung wash outdoors, letting the clothes hang for two or three days. When she brought them into her small cabin to dry over the stove, the clothes would be stiff as boards.

An Indian couple, the Davids, had invited us to go upriver with them in their boat to the new sawmill, where tree stumps, lumber and sawdust covered the earth.

Jonathan David had shaded his eyes with his cap visor, handling the boat with energy. He was a wiry, short man with no front teeth. As he turned the bend, he said, squinting, "Indians lived around here in tents in the winter with a fire in the middle. They used to run barefoot in the snow, then warm their feet by standing on the branches to change socks."

His wife, Rose, had a dark, sunburned face, lighter in shade where her kerchief covered her cheeks. A woman weathered by circumstances, her expression was soft and giving. Two generations ago a woman wore dentalium shells or beads strung through her nose and ears, with tattoo lines on her chin, the bridge of her nose or the outer edge of each eye toward the top of the ear. This latter mark was a sign of mourning, and Old Alice at Nenana and "Captain" Annie at Minto were the last two women to bear those marks.

Rose made us coffee on her Yukon stove that was set outdoors in the grass. The blue smoke from her rusty stack went skyward.

Wild rays of the late sun bombarded the hillsides as the spruce boughs chafed in the wind. Fabian Carey, my trapper friend, sprawled on the grass outside the cabin, surrounded by circle of men talking about trapping and hunting. He trapped fifty miles out of Minchumina at Carey Lake, named after him. He could hunt moose and run on snowshoes like an Indian, and the other men respected that.

"Indians in the early days," said Jonathan David, "used to make the bear angry so he would charge. They tracked it down; sometimes they sang bear songs.

"They used to kneel down on the ground, pointing the spear at the bear's heart." Jonathan David lifted an imaginary spear and held it in front of himself as a soldier would a bayonet. He did not rest the spear on the earth, because the force of the bear would drive it into the earth and then he could not draw it out.

When the bear stood on its hind legs, the hunter would still hold onto the spear, avoiding the bear's swinging, crushing paws as it fought madly, getting more and more cut up by the spear until it dropped dead.

A bearskin was often used as a door covering, symbolizing the valor of the hunter. The Indian hunters told us how they tramped around on snowshoes looking for a glaze of ice, the product of bear-breath vapor. Then they quietly poked a spear into the den hole until they touched the flesh of the bear. The hunter then rammed his spear down, leaning on it with all his weight, as the sleeping bear heaved in torment, lifting the hunter in the air.

I was content to sit there drinking coffee with Rose, listening to the men talk about bears. Most of the bears I have encountered in thirty-three years of Alaskan living have been considerate creatures intent upon their own business of continuing along their own trail. They never charged me; I never got close enough to look them in the eye. I was fortunate, since many people have been maimed, mauled and killed by bears. Bears were a common sight at the gold mine in the wilderness where we once lived. Many times while out blueberry picking I would come across a pile of steaming, large bear stool. My husband, Joe, urged me to rattle a tin can full of rocks to scare away bears and, if that failed, to climb a tree. He had encountered many bears across a creek at the gold mine, and the noisy can worked for him. He never carried a gun, and neither did the other miners; however, when a bear became a nuisance and charged through the cook house, breaking walls and slashing canned stuff, he was shot and his hide was nailed to the cabin.

I can recognize bear smell now. An old Indian woman told me to make an offering of berries to the bear, then sing, and slowly, never running, make my way back.

Rose and I liked bear meat, but I had never scraped or tanned bear skin, I just made bear stew. The old women used to boil bears' feet for hours to make them palatable. Pregnant Indian women were forbidden to eat bear, look at it or sleep on bear skin. Before bear hunting it was good to avoid sexual relations because "the animals would know if a man had been around women too much."

In early days, if a man so much as stepped on a bear's bones on the trail, he would have bad luck. Such had been the Indian taboos. Nowadays the women of Minto enjoyed bear meat, especially bear fat, when it was available, and guns instead of spears made the hunt less threatening. Even beaver meat, formerly taboo for women, was now eaten. Not only were the old Indian taboos changing in Minto but their roots were about to be pulled apart in a major upheaval.

CHAPTER 3

New Minto

The first thing a child will look for to see [whether] you have any food for him when you come back late after dark is to look for blood on your moccasins. If there is no blood on your moccasins, it's disheartening and it's hard to explain to the child and to the rest of the family that you came back empty-handed.

RICHARD FRANK OF MINTO

SOON after government housing was built in New Minto, I visited the village. I found the new location to be beautiful, with an open view of distant hills surrounded by forests, rivers and numerous lakes, sloughs and bogs. Tall spruce spread out beyond the bluffs, an emerald valley of rolling hills and a brown-and-mauve tundra. Every family knew the flats and had a favorite place to hunt and fish. But roads and "inroads" (how apt a word) were being constructed. Heavy equipment was being used to install water pipes and sewers, which eventually froze every winter, causing new problems.

Rose David now had a car and a snowmobile in addition to the old dog sled, and teenagers drove pickup trucks, with water cans to be filled, down the main street. The new government house, shoe-box style, was built up on pilings, with crawl space underneath allowing the forty-below-zero ice freeze to seep up through the flimsy floorboards.

New caches containing meat, fish and berries were built out of plywood instead of logs.

The Davids' log cabin in the old village used to be cool in the summer and warm in the winter when snow was banked around the old cabin; now their house was hot in the summer and cold in the winter. I wondered why the people were not consulted on housing policy. Rose David's white linoleum was hard to clean without running water; the pipes had frozen a year ago and the Davids were back to packing water again. They had electricity as well as satellite TV, but the rates were exorbitant for villagers, many of whom had no jobs.

I met Rose David in Richard Frank's house, where he had a little store that sold eggs, jam, fruit, potatoes and pilot bread. "We are used to white man's food now," said Rose, greeting me. "If the store runs out of pilot crackers, the kids don't know what to do."

Rose had a slight palsy but was the same friendly woman I remembered. She had ten grandchildren now, and when I asked how she liked New Minto, she summed it up: "What can we do? We moved. The floors are cold in winter and people get rheumatism. With the new road all kinds of people come here too."

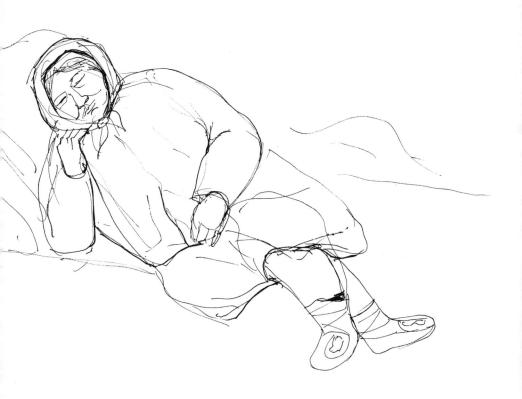

Rose was referring to the fact that a killer was loose in the forest near Minto. For the past year the newspaper had been full of stories about an unidentified murderer who had raped and mutilated six Indian girls, leaving their bodies in the woods. There were no clues until one girl escaped and described the man, whereupon the police traced him to a place close to Minto.

Susy W. Charlie walked slowly across the road, leaning on her cane, her long gray braid swinging. She still went berry picking and did her own housework. Tiny dried spruce needles were stuck in her pierced ears, "to keep them open," explained her granddaughter Jennie. Susy, slightly deaf, spoke broken English but fluent Athabaskan to Jennie, who understood the language but could not speak it. I called Susy Charlie "Sitsu" and urged Jennie's daughter Linda to use the name, which meant grandmother. Usually the children refer to almost everyone as aunt, uncle, cousin or grandparent (such are the close bonds of blood and marriage), but hardly anyone under twenty-five speaks the language fluently.

The Charlies had thirteen great-grandchildren and seven grandchildren, who kept them supplied with fish and moose, helped them with chores and took them for boat rides. A grandchild ran over to Susy and put her arms around her neck while Susy whispered to her in her native tongue. Susy was not stuck away in a home for the aged, but lived in the midst of village life.

She probably had an easier life than her grandmother, who had traveled with a small band, following the caribou in winter and the fish in summer, carrying her baby on top of her heavy pack, pulling the sled herself if there was no dog.

In addition to child rearing and cooking, a woman such as Susy's grandmother was responsible for tanning and sewing all the family's clothing, hauling water, making baskets, weaving the netting on snowshoes, sewing birch bark on canoes, gathering spruce pitch, pitching canoe seams with gum, making nets, taking up fish from nets, cleaning fish, making snares for rabbits, snaring animals, helping to build the home and skinning beaver and mink in camp.

Her man walked with bow and arrow, free to hunt. In those days the Indians harvested the forest produce just as fishermen netted food from the ocean. The land was theirs to roam.

Susy's husband, Jimmie, born in 1893, sat hunched over his cane, casually crossing his long legs. A dark cap shielded his tanned face,

smooth except for a few laugh lines around his eyes. He chewed meat with his own teeth and was alert, although slightly deaf. I had to shout into his ears; like his wife, he refused to wear a hearing aid. Although he never attended school, he was able to read and write.

Jimmie was a former chief and was proud of the three potlatches he had given in his lifetime in Minto. He had given away everything he had owned, once for his mother, once for his first wife and then for his brother-in-law. He had worked at roadhouses and on riverboats and had trapped and hunted. He still recalled how to make birch-bark canoes and had made one for the University of Alaska Museum. I asked him what else birch was used for. Drawing a cigarette from the pack in his shirt pocket, he answered, "Snowshoes, sleds, toboggans and baskets."

I asked him if he went with his wife to collect the birch bark. "In the springtime I used to go. It's easy to peel off the tree then."

He did not have the dull face the old sometimes get from boredom. He was ready to laugh at everything, infecting me with his good humor. He jumped like a young boy when a horsefly bit me, and he ran quickly into the house, returning with a can of Off, which he liberally sprayed. I could hardly believe that he was in his nineties.

I asked him his secret for long life.

"I done everything." His eyes twinkled.

"Everything?" I laughed and he laughed with me.

"I hope you both live to be well over a hundred," I wished them as I left. The secret seemed to be his light enjoyment of life.

Walter Titus, another elder of Minto, is a short, thin man who wears thick bifocals. He and his wife, Louise, used to visit us when they came to Fairbanks to sell her birch-bark baskets. When she died, Walter continued to visit us occasionally.

"We didn't need money when I was a boy," said Walter. "My father trapped for a living. I was brought up like that. There was no way to work for wages till the war. Then I got work on the railroad." Some Indians clung to the old way of life, hunting and trapping, while other men worked for wages on the railroad, on riverboats or woodcutting. Some men did both.

"A long time ago Indians shared everything. Things are changing. The boys make money, they can't share everything anymore. The young men want cars and things for themselves. The boys work for wages on the pipeline, but where does the money go?"

Where indeed? I shook my head in sympathy. Money was treated as a stroke of good fortune to be spent, not to be saved and spread out over the year as some white men did. People were considered rich when they were good hunters and trappers and had lots of furs.

"My father was born in Minto," said Walter, drinking coffee. "He used to go away from the village and come home just before Christmas, and the house was just the way he left it. Now our windows are broken, everything gone. Bad things have happened lately. It is our place, our land to keep clean. It's where our living comes from. White people come and shoot, leave moose here, leave duck there."

I asked Walter what the most important thing was that he thought children should know. "First thing I tell a boy is how to build a fire, to take matches, knife and ax with him in the woods," he replied thoughtfully. "Before matches, people took a stick, made many cuts like slivers. He lit the end and waved it in the air back and forth to make smoke until he got to the next camp. If the fire went out they made a new one with fungus, dry like powder, and fire drill."

Long ago, smoke signals were made with green spruce branches. Continuous smoke far off meant caribou, and if men were out hunting and saw lots of black smoke coming from camp, they knew something was wrong. In winter, they stuck a stick in the snow, the top of which was wrapped with birch bark and moss. If a wolf approached the camp, the stick was thrust into the fire. The blaze frightened the animal away.

"I tell the boys, 'Don't be careless,' " said Walter. " 'Don't swim after eating. Don't go out too far. Don't swim across the river. Think and be careful when handling a gun'—things like that. I tell them to be good to everyone. Treat them like you want to be treated."

"What do they do when they are caught in the dark and cold away from home?" I asked Walter.

"Find a high snowdrift and burrow into it, line it all around with spruce branches."

"What do girls learn?" I asked.

"Girls have to sew, make baskets, bake bread, make slippers, take care of babies, find berries and roots," he replied.

"Then how come so many women are good shots and trappers?" I asked.

Walter smiled.

When I left Walter's house I ran into Richard Frank, whom I had admired ever since I stood at the finish line in the North American Sled Dog Races and saw him come in first, running and pushing behind his dogs, suffering with a high fever the whole grueling trip. He was hospitalized with pneumonia afterward, but he never gave up—a very tough man.

Later he broke his own record in the twenty-mile Tok Race, a record still unbeaten. Richard is not the kind of man one would pick out of a crowd; he is not big and blustery, but a slender man who could walk through a forest and be mistaken for a tree. He has the appearance of a woodsman, yet he calls himself a "river man." Richard began as a cabin boy with the Yutana Barge Line at fifteen and stayed twenty-two years as a river pilot on the steamboat.

A former chief of Minto, he has had as many careers as four men, yet he is only in his early fifties. His bone-ridged face is distinguished by black eyes framed by short black hair, now turning gray. His wife, Anna, works for the Tanana chiefs and is a deacon in the Episcopal Church.

"I saw my first white man on the Ray River when I was a young boy out trapping with my family," Richard said. Because of the family's nomadic life he never went past the sixth grade.

"The land is the only thing we have to fall back on when nothing else works," said Richard. "If you kill off all the animals, they can't be replaced. The land that's been damaged by oil cannot be rebuilt. These are the things we fear would be lost forever."

Richard is rooted in Athabaskan tradition, and one of his favorite subjects is the moose hunt. "We get up at four o'clock in the morning. Anna makes me some strong tea with sugar. Maybe we pack some pilot bread and some dried meat. That's all. We make tea out there, we don't take much with us. By six o'clock we're out on the trail on snowshoes, looking for fresh moose tracks. We can hear the moose coming; he sounds like a tank coming through the brush. We follow him, and every once in a while he stops and browses and looks around. Sometimes the snow is belly high. Sometimes fifty below.

"The hardest thing to do is run after the moose until he is tired out. We try to get him to run in circles so he won't get too far from home and we have to carry it back. We are trained to be good runners on snowshoes." Snowshoe running can be torture, every step agony; yet aching sinews are part of trail life.

Richard said with authority, "After we have shot it, we point the head toward home. We never, never let a wounded moose go, even if it takes a week to get him," he emphasized. "I try to teach my son to hunt the old way, on an empty belly—just give him salt, tea, sugar and matches. If he had wounded a moose, he had to go right back without eating what was on the table and track it down. He had to learn that meat for us was to live." Richard looked at me to see if I understood.

"The biggest part of our money now goes for meat in white men's stores. We are used to meat, that's what we've been brought up on. If we can't get moose we have to buy beef in the stores. The backbone of the moose is the choicest part, given to the old people. That bone is so large, it hangs over the plate. I've never had it yet."

Richard's eyes sobered. "We have to share the meat. Part is given to elders, part for the potlatch, and the rest divided equally among the families of Minto. If someone got a moose and did not give it away, we would send someone over to ask him why."

When a family doesn't get a moose in the fall, it is like the city supermarket without meat on the shelves for six months, because moose is the main staple.

Today there are many problems with hunting in the area. Walter had told me, "White men are all over the land we hold by right. For fifteen miles around our village, we hunt rats [muskrats] and moose. We always did. Now there are over twenty-four camps there. Everywhere you turn you are bumping into a white man.

"We have airplane and Sno-go [snowmobile] hunters in here all winter hunting our game. My friend went up to his trap line; every beaver had been trapped by airplane. He didn't want to trap them all, so he let them go. When he went back they were gone. They shoot fox and wolf from the planes, and the trapper that goes with dogs don't have a chance," he said.

"We found one whole moose just rotting. I don't think it's right for a man to use airplane and come here. Shoot moose, cut off a little piece and horns, and leave the rest to rot. Go down to the fish camp and leave his garbage."

The new road brought town hunters by car, truck and camper to compete with Indian hunters for the game. No wonder Chief Peter John of Minto was protesting. It was not illegal for other men to hunt at Minto. However, the Indians took pride in the fact that they were hunters and have always subsisted on wild meat, while the white man, who can afford to buy meat in town, is practically stealing the Indians' meat from their land.

Wallace Olsen, who lived among Athabaskans, knew a man who came to hunt at Minto on weekends. The man followed Bureau of Wildlife Preservation fish and game restrictions and did not feel that Indians should have special privileges. He told Olsen: "The people gave up their hunting rights when they took the money for their land. They want to have the land, the money and all their rights besides. Well, they can't. They have to follow the rules like everyone else now. They sold out their way of life.

"They can have my camp," he continued, "but all I'm going to leave is a pile of ashes. I say give them the land, on one condition: no more B.I.A., no more welfare, no more free medical care, no more pampering them. They want the land to live on, well, let them live on it, but don't ask me to pay taxes to support them!"

Such angry statements indicate that the land claims settlement has become an emotional question, bringing to the surface many feelings and tensions that have built up over long periods.

The traditional moose hunt came under the scrutiny of the Alaska supreme court in the case against Carlos Frank, a relative of Richard's, who transported a cow moose out of season for the ceremonial funeral potlatch. Many felt that Indians should be treated like everyone else and should follow fish and game regulations. The courts, after a four-year debate, decided that Carlos Frank and other Athabaskan villagers were protected by constitutional guarantees of freedom of religion to hunt moose out of season if necessary. "It's a religious act," Richard Frank told me. "The old people told the hunters to go and get moose for the potlatch." It was a landmark case and a victory for Indians.

Richard, whose life had changed from woodsman, trapper, hunter and dog racer to soldier in the South Pacific and river pilot, to president of the Native Association, president of the Minto Corporation and one of the Tanana chiefs directing the flow of thousands of dollars through the land claims act, stated the dilemma of the Indians simply: "We were taught to hunt and trap. The law said we had to go to school and learn how to read and write. Our whole culture is changing and we are trying hard to hold on to it and go with modern progress at the same time."

Richard's ancestors used to memorize explanations of natural phenomena, which also instructed them how to live. Today the young people have little knowledge of their tradition. But there is a deep, often inarticulate, hunger to learn. In spite of a large gap between generations, the last few years have seen a resurgence of Native peoples trying to discover their roots. There is an urgency to capture this oral history and language before the old people die and the link between the past and present is gone forever.

One of the remaining important traditions I had long heard about and yearned to attend was the potlatch ceremony. Before I left Minto, Rose invited me to attend a potlatch to be given months later. It was an honor to be invited and I promised to attend.

CHAPTER 4

Chief Peter John
of Minto

I tell you that we are people . . . on the go, and I believe if we were put in one place, we should die off like rabbits . . . I ask you not to let the white people come near us. Let us live our own lives in the customs we know.

CHIEF ALEXANDER OF TOLOVANA, *1915,*
at first chiefs meeting with U.S. government
representative Judge James Wickersham,
Alaska's delegate to Congress

The mink was plentiful, and so was the fox, beaver and otter. People used to make a lot of money from fur in the Minto Flats area . . . Today you don't even see fur signs anyplace . . . An airplane was flying just about a mile from us, he was circling back and forth, and it landed there before we could get over to them, and they killed two moose right ahead of us. They just took off from Fairbanks that morning, after about thirty minutes of flying . . . after it took me thirteen hours to hunt and track moose, they killed them two moose.

CHIEF PETER JOHN OF MINTO, *1966*

THE first time I met Chief Peter John was on a painting trip to Tanana. Mrs. Jimmie, the lead Minto dancer, had introduced me, saying I was an artist.

My first impression was of a proud, burly, barrel-chested man. I said I was glad to meet the chief of Minto. He corrected me, saying, "We are not called the chief, because 'the chief' means something else."

I muttered that I did not know that and something to the effect that I would like to paint him sometime, feeling that he would never sit still for me.

Eleven years were to pass before I painted him. I had asked another villager if he thought the chief would pose for me, then sent a note to be delivered to him at Minto, asking if he would sit for a portrait, making it clear that I was giving it to the university.

When I arrived, Chief Peter John was sitting on the shady side of his house. He was blocky, a gray-haired man emanating great purpose and physical well-being. His face was square, heavy-jawed and deeply bronzed, with a straight, short nose. Thick brows accented high cheekbones, and his left eye had a perpetual squint from facing sun and snow and scanning distances without sunglasses. His broad face was unlined except for a few laugh lines around his penetrating black eyes. He was seventy-five, but could have easily passed for fifty-five.

He directed me to a chair a few feet away on the grass. "Why didn't you ask me if you could come and paint me?"

I answered that I had met him eleven years ago, and I didn't think he would remember me. I did not tell the truth, that I was afraid of a refusal.

Many people have come to the village to ask him favors—politicians, anthropologists, linguists, government land surveyors, engineers, fishermen and hunters, and an occasional artist like myself.

I asked what I should call him. "Call me anything," he said as he crossed his legs comfortably and sized me up. "I'm not really a chief, not exactly. They call me that, but I am not like the old chiefs used to be. Their job was to take care of their people. It was different in those days. A chief, a real chief, gives a potlatch by himself."

Nonetheless, he had represented the Minto people as an elder chief as long as I could remember. (In addition, there was an elected village council.) Peter John read current magazines and newspapers and was thoroughly conversant with federal and state programs. The

people had implicit trust in his ability to make decisions for the future of the village.

He invited me into his house, one of the new modern government houses, similar to the others. It was a simple house, containing a Yukon stove and a propane stove in the kitchen area and two bedrooms.

On the wall was an enlarged photograph of the chiefs, taken in 1915 in Fairbanks. He named the chiefs for me, and I think he was surprised that I knew all their names and where they came from.

The chiefs had posed stiffly for their portraits, with stern expressions. Chief Alexander William wore a suit; others wore beaded moose-hide jackets with dentalium around their necks. All had modern haircuts and trading-post shirts and pants.

The other chiefs were William of Tanana, Thomas of Nenana, Charlie of Minto, Alexander of Tolovana and Ivan of Koschakat. Paul Williams of Tanana was the interpreter in the photo.

Peter John's wife, Elsie, was a granddaughter of Chief Ivan (pronounced E-van), who was one of the most influential chiefs of the lower Tanana. In the photograph, Chief Ivan, whose Indian name was Kruzah, wore a fringed moose-hide jacket heavily beaded down the front opening, with dentalium worn as a necklace and over his shoulder, attached to a knife sheath at his side. His broad face had a determined expression, and his powerful hands gripped his knees. The photo was taken at the first meeting of the chiefs with United States government representatives, Judge Wickersham of Alaska and the railroad men.

At the meeting the officials tried to put the Indians on a reservation, but the chiefs all emphatically refused. Ivan said, "I have heard that the United States government was supposed to be a good government . . . they even protect dogs in the streets. And if the government is able to protect dogs in the street, it should be able to look out for us."

Chief Ivan was a powerful man, a friend of the Russians. He had saved the life of a Russian trader who had incurred the emnity of the Indians. The trader's wife had been killed and the Russian was about to be killed when Ivan interceded.

The chief and his men had fed and helped white men, among them Lieutenant Henry T. Allen, who wrote later how he met Ivan's party camped on the Yukon with forty birch canoes fastened to the shore and an abundance of king salmon split and hung up over the water. "Their surroundings," Lieutenant Allen wrote in 1887, "were luxurious when compared to ours. It seemed that we had never seen bedding look so clean and comfortable, or the colors of calico so fresh." The chief's following consisted of seventy-five people, who fed Lieutenant Allen's men and "sent them on their way with fresh vigor and supplies."

It was a typical story of white men's dependence upon Indians, for they knew little about subsisting on the land and would have died from starvation or from frostbite in the bitter subarctic winters if the Indians hadn't helped them.

I asked Chief Peter John if he would sit for the painting dressed in his moose-hide jacket. His wife had tanned the skins and fringed the sleeves and the band across the chest; above a row of porcupine-quill stitchery was a beaded feather. "My wife is the only one here who can still do quillwork," said Peter John.

Elsie was a dignified, frail woman with her hair knotted at the back, and her face seemed grief-stricken as she set about making coffee. She seemed to be suffering from some pain or worry.

I had chosen the hottest day of the year. The chief sat outdoors, completely at ease; he saw no reason not to begin. I would have liked to stall—I wanted to know him better. But he was ready, so I plunged right in. Setting my heavy oil box on another chair, I began to squeeze out a full range of oil colors on my palette.

"I don't have all that many colors on me," the chief noted. He had put on his prized dentalium necklace. In the early days such necklaces were traded for a stack of furs—usually only chiefs could afford them. Throughout the years I had saved dentalium shells. Now I gave a small packet of them to the chief, who passed them to his wife.

The chief's face was strong, the countenance of a man who had come to terms with himself, with his generation and with his people. He was in his own rightful place; it was an accepting face.

I would not have been able to approach him so readily eleven years ago. He seemed different, possessed of an inner glow, a happiness I had not seen in anyone for a long time. I tried to remember what it reminded me of but could not. His eyes were penetrating. I had him turn slightly so that I could concentrate on painting his face.

We talked about the old chiefs and Indian life in the past. "They were not like us," he said. "They used to kill black bear and grizzlies with a spear. Just stand there and wait. That's the kind of Indians we were a long time ago. Not somebody you can kick around and say you can't do anything. They were like those Olympic runners. They were strong, run fast. We don't see runners like that today."

Elsie brought out some coffee for us in thick mugs.

"When I was younger I ran ahead of dogs to Nenana, in the winter, before the snow got deep. I used to run thirty miles," he said. He ran on snowshoes over difficult terrain, ran game to the ground and snowshoed all day without food in temperatures of fifty below zero, like his ancestors. He also had the reputation of being a champion wrestler.

"Other men are just as important," he stressed modestly, trying to explain to me how he felt as one with them, that he was not any better or higher than the others in the village. He wanted to impress that on me, to make sure I understood.

I roughed out his head on the canvas and began to paint. "My wife is a good hunter," he continued. "She shot a bear. It was right in front of her." He motioned that the space between her and the bear was as close as between him and me. "She was out of shells, so I helped. She's a good shot. She goes with me when I hunt." I wondered who had shot that bear. Perhaps that was his way of praising his wife, who watched quietly.

"It was a grizzly," he said, answering my question. "I've shot so many bears and moose, I can't keep count."

As he spoke I noticed his short, blunt fingers. They were like his conversation, directly to the point, unwavering as his eyes upon mine.

It was useless to ask him to look the other way. The portrait was coming along, but I was not the master of it.

I was doing my best, but the hot, sweltering sun had moved on me. It was over ninety degrees, yet I was too intent to move my chair, the paints or the chief, so I continued.

"I'm married fifty years," Peter John said, looking fondly at Elsie. "I knew all the chiefs in my lifetime. Chief Charlie's brother was smarter than he was. I went to the mission school for two years, but I didn't learn anything, so I taught myself to read and write."

He kept squinting with his right eye. I found it impossible to mix the exact shade of his skin, which was a dark, sunburned, warm coppery brown.

I don't know how long we sat in the sun until I finally stopped, having gone as far with the painting as I could. I thanked him and asked if I could put the wet oil painting behind his stove for safekeeping.

Peter John solved the problems in the village with charismatic leadership. "I never believe what a man tells me about another. I like to ask the man himself, like a trial. I ask him to his face if it was like that. Then I listen to the other man and other people. That's the way the chiefs used to do it. It makes trouble in the village if you don't."

He was a religious man who believed in God and attended the Episcopal Church and occasionally the Assembly of God. When Bishop Cochran, head of the Episcopal Church in Alaska, came to Minto, the men prayed together.

This year the Johns lost their only son. "I never cried for my son, Orion, when he died," said Chief Peter John. "People came to the house, but I never cried. It was the Lord's will." Looking at Elsie's face, I now perceived her sorrow. He asked me about my parents and I told him that they were dead, that I had missed going to my father's funeral in New York, unable to get there in time. They had already buried Orion and put a tombstone on his grave, but they would not be released from grief until they gave the potlatch—the Indian way.

A gray bird hovered about Peter John, not lighting on him but seeming to. I looked startled. He replied that birds often sat on his arms, shoulders, knees and head. Immersed in wilderness, he had inherited an affinity for animals and birds of the forest. He was like a strong spruce with the sap still in him—birds liked to be around him. "Not the ducks," he said. "They know I am hungry for them and they don't come to me."

Peter John had fought hard for land claims. "We did not get

enough of our land," he said. "We did not get our mineral rights."
Senator Ernest Gruening said that Chief Peter John was one of the first
to be active in calling attention to the land claims and that he was a
pioneer deserving a great deal of credit.

"Lots of things have happened to me in my life. I saw my first
white man in 1912. In Minto I saw my first electricity, first Christmas
tree, my first airplane. Lots of changes. Me and my wife, we had lots
of kids. Some died—no doctor in those days. We went hungry lots of
times. My wife nearly died three times—she had pneumonia.

"Young people don't follow old ways anymore. I been brought up
in the old Indian way. I hunt and trap, never drink. It's hard work. Lots
of times I come home without anything, children waiting hungry." He
looked at me and paused. "My father's last words to me were 'Help
people all you can and take care of yourself—no one else will.' "

In memory of his only son, Orion, Peter John wrote a song for the
potlatch to be held in August, and he translated it for me.

>All the love that he showed us
>We can never pay it back.
>
>And with his voice,
>His songs and his guitar,
>He would have made more friends.
>
>He was the best hunter and trapper.
>I taught him all that I knew.
>
>We will never see him hunt or trap again.
>We will miss him in all the things
>That he used to say and do.

"Orion was a good boy. We adopted him," his wife said. "He died
of whiskey."

What were Peter John's thoughts of his son, who had died frozen,
unconscious in the snow? I remembered a story the minister's wife had
told me about Orion. One of the best hunters in the village, Orion was
gone about four days on his trap line, when a snowstorm began over
Minto Flats. The weather got colder, dropping to twenty below. All
Orion had was his backpack and sleeping bag, so he decided to wait
out the storm, sleeping in a snowbank.

Peter John, upset because Orion was overdue, called Al Wright,
the pilot, and told him, "I don't care how long it takes or what it costs.
Find him."

Al circled the flats until he spotted Orion's foot tracks in the snow. He could not stop without getting stuck in the soft snow, so he shouted, "When I come by, throw your bedroll in, and when I come by again, get in."

His plane, equipped with skis, taxied in a circle. First time around, Orion threw in his bedroll and backpack, and when the plane came by again, he climbed in, shivering from the cold. He survived then because his father had taught him how, but his father could not teach him how to handle alcohol, because it had not been part of his culture.

Peter John shook his head. "Orion liked to hunt and trap, but most young people don't want to. They don't want the old ways; they are working for money. They don't listen to me."

"But a lot of the Indian ways are coming through you to affect other people who meet you," I answered. "It's not all lost."

The chief got up early, went to bed early, never joining the men who stayed up all night and slept all day. He made his living trapping and hunting, not working for wages. As one man in the village said, "He got more fur on snowshoes than others did with snowmobiles."

Peter John's wife moved her thin arms as she sewed a pair of beaded moccasins. I noticed that she did everything the chief asked. When I questioned whether she let Peter John have his way in everything, she did not answer. Peter John answered for her: "If she does not agree, she won't say anything."

About the upcoming potlatch, she said, "We try to get rid of our sorrow. Six people will share giving it. It will be a big potlatch. We give away rifles, blankets, shirts, socks, moccasins, whatever people need and whatever we have."

Peter John told me that he had seen a lot of medicine men in his lifetime. "Medicine men had lots of power, they cured people. I saw them cut out a tumor. Once I heard of a man that come back from the dead after ten days."

"In those days they had to cure people," I replied. "There were no doctors. No one else could do it." There is still no doctor at Minto, and if someone is seriously ill he has to go to Fairbanks.

"There was a war in the seventeen hundreds right here in this spot," said Peter John. "The Arctic Village Indians came down and made war. They walked with bow and arrow. Made war to get even— somebody killed a relative, I guess."

His grandson showed me old arrowheads taken from the area. They were shiny like glass, but I didn't know what material they were made from, probably obsidian.

When I visited them the next day, the chief and his family were sitting under a makeshift canvas, an overhang against sun and rain. His wife sat gracefully, her legs tucked under her, beading a moccasin to be given away at the potlatch. Her grieved expression relaxed as she threaded the needle.

Their daughter joined us in the shade with her knitting. Earlier, as I had strolled by her house, I saw her rocking her baby, who was swaddled into a homemade hammock fastened near the windows.

As the women were doing their work, I took out my pad and pen. It was a good place to sit and sketch. Peter John's face continued to elude me, and my sketch, I thought, had too many shadows, but his grandson liked the resemblance.

Later that evening I remembered what his smile had reminded me of: the face of an ancient Buddha sculpture I had seen in the Seattle Art Museum. The chief's head had nobility and dignity, a sense that he was contributing to traditional Indian life. Not many men can sit on their land, survey hundreds of miles of wilderness—lakes, swamps, rivers, hills and mountains—and feel a continuity of spirit, knowing that their ancestors had fished, hunted and bathed in the same streams.

As I stood on the deck of *The Yukon,* I recalled Peter John's face and words while the boat eased its way past Old Minto. My efforts to paint the chief were a continuation of the thread that connected my life with those of the people of the river.

CHAPTER 5

On the Tanana River

People in villages met them with willow branches as a sign of peace. Innumerable flocks of swallows nesting on sandy cliffs flew over . . . Winds brought the smell of forest fires . . . Beaver were at work everywhere and bears gambolled on banks.

LIEUTENANT L. A. ZAGOSKIN,
explorer with the Russian
Trading Company, 1842

THE day was bleak and a dull haze hung in the air, draining the gold color from the trees. The tug jolted and leaped in a little dance, its bottom stuck in mud on a sand bar. *The Yukon* heaved like an oceangoing liner, and there she remained on a hump. She had been stuck in the same place since six o'clock that morning. I could see the tug moving, working water under the stationary barge.

On the river time passed slowly. It took so long to do every little thing. I felt as if I had been aboard for weeks instead of days. At home I used energy to rush around, and at the end of the day, time always seemed too short for all the things I had left to do. Here time stretched out before me like an endless winding river. My face reflected my tranquility, happy to be surrounded by wilderness again, mirroring the waterways.

Finally the boat moved on and we passed a place called Swan's Neck, below Tolovana Slough. The wide river is curved like a swan's neck. "Constantly changing here," said the captain, turning the wheel. "Swans used to nest here."

"My father drowned here," said Adriana, sadly dropping her husky voice. "We don't know but think it was his heart. He dropped overboard. They never found his body. Rivermen say the Tanana buries its men."

Adriana's father was George Black, the colorful riverboat captain, and she learned about the river at his knee. He loved the wild riverways of interior Alaska and started freighting in 1914, when Indian life was abundant along the Yukon.

He caught typhoid fever one year from the river water. When I thought of his death in the Tanana,* I realized that for a riverboat captain, he died a fitting death in this broad, silty river.

The river looked deceiving. The sounding boat, a runabout with an outboard motor, curved away to one end of the mile-wide river to check the river's depth. It was too shallow and the captain had to back out.

"Tanana River bottom is mud; the Yukon is gravel," said Adriana, brushing away a fly. "That's why when you get stuck on the Yukon you really have problems." The tug did a complete slow turnaround to churn up the mud. The propellers on the bottom of the tug washed out their own channel.

Fireweed's magenta stems were massed everywhere along the banks. Birches leaped like sunlight from the hillsides, black birds flashed among their white stems.

The barge was stuck in McKinley Crossing for three hours with the engines running. The vibrations went through my ears to every part of my body. To cure an earache, anthropologist Cornelius Osgood wrote, the Indians used to burn the distal end of a ground squirrel's tail, allowing smoke to enter the ear. O for a distal end!

It was a hard, cold, forbidding country we surveyed. The vast landscape of sky, water and land was a changing frame for a painter. The wind and snow must howl and storm all winter in these flatlands.

"We'll all give a sigh of relief to get to the Yukon, where the river is deeper," remarked Adriana.

*Dené, tená, dená, taná, are all dialect variations of the root word meaning "the people." Na is a suffix indicating "river." Thus Tanana is "the river of the people."

Perhaps I could have paddled this river by canoe, stopping to paint on shore? My paint box alone would sink the canoe, a metal sixteen- by twenty-inch box loaded with oil paints, canvases and brushes. And where would I set all the wet canvases to dry?

I longed to immerse myself in the wilderness, to roll in the wild grasses and to brush my sides along the spruces. Growing earth nurtured me like a parched crop that receives rain. However, it was enough to watch the changing vistas of hills and clouds, to observe the patterns and harmonies of nature from the deck and to feel the wind and weather. The fragrance of the forest leaves was a cleansing force; I needed and hungered for it. A flight of ducks opened out in the morning sun over the valley in a burst of silver wings.

Ray, the engineer, said the engine was turned off last night. The noise I heard was only the generator! The boat continued to weave and work back and forth to loosen the mud in order to glide free. We had been stuck at McKinley Crossing for six hours. "It's a bad place. Same place the boat was stuck on last trip," Adriana said. Mount McKinley was invisible, covered with clouds, some of the forms resembling a big bear nuzzling a small bear.

The banks around the bend were undercut with holes, homes of the parka squirrels who rushed about their business, pausing only to look at us. Spruces were full-needled, a blue-green with healthy cones. No permafrost here, no permanently frozen soil to stunt tree growth.

As I stood on the deck of *The Yukon,* I thought of the first people to live here. Anthropologists believe that they came to Alaska over a land bridge that connected Siberia with Alaska. Some believe that as early as forty thousand years ago they followed the caribou migrating through treeless tundra. By 6,000 B.C., interior Alaska was a vast spruce forest populated with a variety of game and fish.

I thought of how the Indians had met the first strangers to their land with willow branches as a sign of peace. I visualized the men and women standing on the banks wearing their traditional moose or caribou skins with the hair inside, shirts reaching to mid-thigh and ending in points front and back. Trousers were a combination of pants and moccasin; large gauntlet mittens were hung from straps over the shoulders; and fur caps covered their heads.

Women's clothing was made the same way, except that the jacket was hung below the knees and cut in rounded fashion. In the summer the skin was worn tanned and without the hair.

Some rich men wore a knife belt suspended from the right shoulder and often decorated with dentalium shells. Upon entering the house, the man would slip off his outer clothes, turn them inside out, hang them in the cold for the perspiration to freeze so that it could be brushed off, and slip into a lighter set of clothes for use indoors. Dentalium shells or porcupine quills were sewn on for decoration.

My reverie of early Indians halted abruptly as the boat shook and we were unglued. It had taken ten hours of patient working with a boat alongside of the barge, pumping water under her stern to loosen the barge from the tight mud. In appreciation the sun burst out in full glory, selecting a stand of straight spruce over one hundred feet tall —perfect for cabin logs.

The hillsides were a mass of lacy trees, a mosaic of fall lemons, pale limes, oranges and dark greens. Indians had used trees for medicine, heating the gum of spruce sap and resin to spread over cuts and burns. To cure a stomachache they boiled spruce needles all day and gave a spoonful of the warm broth to the patient, and for throat problems they boiled the fibers of spruce bark to make a paste. Willow, cottonwood and alder bark were used for excessive bleeding after childbirth: according to Cornelius Osgood, the anthropologist, women took a hot bath in the boiled juices.

My bones ached. I wondered what the Indians did for that. My old mattress had seen much river life. The gamy, pungent scent of highbush cranberries and bog blueberries floated up to the wheelhouse from the woods. Sun sparkled on the river and pork roast wafted through the vent leading to the messhall.

At the table we discussed the future of Alaska. I said I feared that the oil people would own Alaska in a few years. "They're biding their time now. They want our offshore leases. They are building ships, freighters, icebreakers, laying the groundwork. Their men are getting in our legislature."

Captain Peterson shrugged and admitted that new oil buildings were going up in Anchorage. "Anchorage will be the oil capital of Alaska," he said.

"Maybe a dam will be built and the railroad will be extended," added Adriana. "Alaska will be greatly changed."

I nodded my head regretfully, looking at the inky river. "The pipeline will change Alaska. All the crowds that we came up here to avoid will be on our back doorstep, bringing noise and pollution. Our woods will be full of other people's garbage and beer cans and oil spills in the Arctic. I dread to think of it. I will fight against any large dam being built in Alaska. It would ruin the salmon run and bring heavy industry and resulting smog to our land."

Adriana settled her tall bulk in a chair and said, "It's so sad there is hardly anyone left along the river; it used to be full of people. We delivered freight to Indians and the old-timers in their cabins, to the goldminers and woodcutters."

In the wheelhouse after breakfast, Dave Walker, one of the first Indian river pilots, now with thirty-seven years of experience, took over the wheel and lit up his fourth cigarette of that morning. Dave had accompanied his father on freighting trips in the Iditarod country for mining companies. A lean, gray-haired man of fifty-five, he was completely in control of his feelings.

Adriana filled the coffee cups and passed a plate of freshly baked cookies. "In the late thirties we came down the river and saw huge bonfires at night. Indians camped around, their tents up, salmon drying on the racks. We traded flour and coffee for moose hides, beadwork and furs. Old prospectors lived along the way too. Other men haven't taken their places. It's a hungry land now, nothing here.

"Biggest thrill I had was in June, near rat [muskrat] camp." Adriana stopped for a sip of steaming coffee. "Indians came and met us in their small boats. They'd come down the sloughs around Stevens Village. They'd want gasoline, clothes, food and mail. We'd trade or sell. We had lots of clothes and food for sale, like a trading post. There were some trading posts, but we got there earlier, before the other boats with supplies came. We'd have apples and oranges, too, and they were hungry. They were sure glad to see us come. They named lots of kids after us."

The sun was hazy, engines loud and sweepers low now. I gathered pinecones that had fallen on the deck to decorate my windowsill. The river was thick, silty, nickel-shale color today. The floor of the forest along the river was vermilion, and mushrooms and gray lichen could be seen in black peat.

We picked up a new barge at Manley Hot Springs, pushing a thousand tons now and going slower. The barge tanker was filled with fuel oil, which would be pumped into the village tanks, and the deck-load consisted of pipes, tanks, propane and oil barrels. I could not imagine how it stayed afloat in just five feet of water. A dangerous load of tinder—I hoped the deck hands were not smoking.

Dave Walker went ahead of us in the sounding boat, testing the depth of water in the sluggish, tortuous winding bars and hairpin bends.

"Have you heard about the reputation of the Tanana?" asked Captain Art. "The Tanana is too thick to drink, too thin to plow, ten miles wide and two feet deep!"

At the river bend we passed the old deserted Indian cabins of Coschaket (pronounced "cross jacket" by whites), meaning "mouth of the river." Grasses grew from the sod rooftops, and doors and windows gaped, part of the mysterious unwritten history buried in the forests.

"October fifth, 1944, we froze in at Coschacket," said the captain as he peered through binoculars. "It used to be a Native village, like Kokrines. Now nothing is there. We just froze in. The water just froze around the boat while we slept. We waited three weeks for a plane to land on skis and get us out. We gave all the food aboard to the Indians, as it would have frozen." The boat had to stay there till ice breakup the next spring.

"On a clear day in Tanana they can see our boat coming from fifty miles away," Captain Art continued. "Caribou used to swim across the river in 1939, before the war. One climbed aboard the barge once. They'd cross between Tanana and Rampart. This place coming up is Caribou Crossing. They had a big slaughter up at Circle. Both Indian and white began to shoot like crazy. After that we never saw such numbers again. Now we don't see any.

"Out of Kantishna River we used to see fish camps, hundreds of fish camps. They got feed for themselves and dogs, but the Department of Fish and Wildlife stopped them." Captain Art handled the wheel passing the mouth of the Kantishna River.

Agnes, the cook, rang the dinner bell for a heavy meal of chicken and gravy, dumplings, peas and carrots, brownies with pecans. Agnes, an attractive thin woman of sixty-three with black hair and gold earrings, had twenty-one grandchildren. She cooked in Alaskan bush style, without fresh foods and with heavy use of fattening baked stuff, in spite of the fact that the larder had salad makings.

We were stuck again on a sand bar to the tempo of throbbing engines. No wonder Adriana called the lookout post Art's "ulcer seat." Agnes, Adriana and I sat apprehensively in the wheelhouse watching the men climb over the barge, testing the water's depth. Two Indian hunters in a riverboat passed us with a moose in the boat. They got stuck on a mud bar too, but shoved off with a paddle.

"If they're stuck, what about us? What chance have we got?" said Adriana.

Captain Art told about Archdeacon Hudson Stuck, whose boat was stranded on a high sand bar on the Tanana River. As the boat passed, the captain inquired, "What's your name?"

The bishop hollered back, "Stuck."

Again the question and again "Stuck."

Finally the captain, exasperated, shouted, "I know you're stuck, but what the hell is your name?"

In the early days the Indians had a fool-proof method for traveling on the rivers in birch-bark canoes. The seams were sewn with roots of spruce and calked with spruce gum. When a leak was discovered, the Indians went ashore, built a fire to warm the spruce gum they carried, rubbed it into the seam and it was watertight again!

I painted on deck with my hair tied in a kerchief, as the wind was blowing hard. We passed a place named Squaw's Crossing. Did a woman walk across here? Had there been a woman's uprising of some sort or a tragic incident involving a woman? No one seemed to know.

A flock of ducks flew against the sunset, looking like a calendar photograph, just too corny to paint. The crew, with much effort and shouting and flinging of ropes, tied up the barge for the night. In the light of a darkling moon I went in peace to bed.

Tomorrow the Yukon at last!

CHAPTER 6

The Yukon

*One unbroken mass of snow-covered
ice. From its source to its mouth. Neither
pen nor pencil can give any idea of the
dreary grandeur, the vast monotony, or
the unlimited expanse we saw before us.*

FREDERICK WHYMPER

THE deck hands mopped the
floors at two o'clock in the morning, and I awoke listening to the water
sloshing under my door. At last we were on the Yukon, a river about
two thousand miles long and one to five miles wide.

For thousands of years men lived along the Yukon, leaving no
recorded history, no written messages, except an occasional flint chip,
a scraper and the bones they gnawed. Their underground shelters had
roofs consisting of poles covered with birch bark, moss and dirt. In the
winter they fished through the ice, using fish spears, lures, bone hooks,
traps and nets set under the ice. They used adzes, picks, bone-fleshing
tools, arrowheads and stone-scraping slabs.

Many Indians remember seeing their first white man on the
Yukon. An old woman reported that as a child she saw three white men
come down the river on a raft. The men made a sign that they were
hungry, pointed to the dried fish on her rack and to their mouths. The

men were traders and they wanted a birch-bark canoe. They offered "little shiny things, yellow things, heavy and round, but the people sent these things from one hand to another hand and an old man threw them away.

"But the next time we saw a white man, every person in the whole village ran into the woods. This priest with bright red hair came," the old woman said. "Nobody ever saw red hair before. One man stayed with arrows and a spear, ready to kill."

We passed a large field of blueberry bushes with black branches and a speckling of yellow leaves, a translucent popsicle color. While passing by, Ray, the engineer, reported, "I saw a bunch of hippies last month on a raft going to Tanana to build a commune. They hung hammocks on the raft, and when the barge passed them, they were running around without clothes." Probably doing the washing . . .

We stopped briefly in Tanana, the junction of the Tanana and Yukon rivers, pulling up alongside another barge, which was loaded with five hundred tons of fuel oil. We were now pushing three barges carrying fuel oil on their hulls and cargo on their decks. It terrified me to think of the combustible mess we were hauling. The deck hands smoked constantly, throwing out their cigarettes just as they leaped from tug to barge. A jeep, tractor and lumber roof supports for a two-million-dollar high school at Nulato were loaded aboard.

At the wheelhouse Captain Art maneuvered the huge tug in darkness and rain. Tanana log cabins were strung out along the banks. The church, new government school and hospital were visible. It had rained all day and the Yukon was rough and choppy. Bright searchlights spotlighted the men handling the freight.

It began to rain again, gray skies casting a sickly greenish pallor on the golden birches. I heard a raven's grating call and watched his glistening form descend. What a tricky character he was in legend— clown, hero, creator and destroyer. I watched him with new respect. A raven was never killed, since he might be a spirit of a dead person and killing him would bring bad luck in hunting.

"It's cooler today," Captain Art said at lunch. "Feels like snow ahead."

"Snow in the hills already," reported Ray. "On the way back upriver the leaves will be dropping fast. Winter is coming." My feet were cold.

Ray gave us, at lunch, his definition of a perfect job—working in a sewerage plant: "Nothing to do all day under antiseptic conditions." He calls this trip "the milk run." With an average of seven to ten children in families, Alaskans buy canned milk by the case. The Arctic pilots I used to fly with called their trips to the radar station in the far north "the beer run."

The Yukon was getting wider, the color of blue slate, not as muddy as the Tanana. Today it was placid, smooth as lake water, with the edge reflecting spruces and a clear full moon.

I had a hot Yukon River shower aboard the boat in the bathroom I shared with the Petersons, which was as large as my whole room. The filtered soft water was luxurious and made my hair feel silken. Bathing Indian fashion along the Yukon was once an exotic experience for foreigners. The Russian explorer Lieutenant Laurenti Ivan Alexiev Zagoskin shared a bath in a small *kashim,* a men's communal house, with forty Indians. Surrounded by Yukon River water, the Indians preferred the steam bath. "I lost my breath from the pungent smell of the urine with which the natives had just washed themselves," wrote Zagoskin in 1842. "I was still a novice. My first reaction was to climb out."

When Peter Freuchen went to Greenland, the Eskimos there used urine to bathe also, and he wrote amusingly of the woman with urine-washed hair whom he took to a dance. There was no soap at that time to cut grease.

In 1833, the Russian Andrei Glazunov was one of the first white men to see Indians along the Yukon and to take a sweat bath with them. At their meeting the Indians shouted, holding bows and arrows. They wore hawk feathers twisted in their long braids and eagle down, grease, spruce gum and red ocher in their hair. (To cut off a man's hair was a deadly insult!) They painted their faces vermilion and wore dentalium ornaments in their pierced noses and necklaces of bears' claws, sable tails, wolf ears, and hawk and eagle feathers.

They invited Glazunov into their communal house. In the light of the fish-oil lamps were over two hundred naked men taking a sweat bath. Glazunov told the Indians that he was interested in trading furs, and he passed out tobacco and snuff. Some of the Indians were so dazed by the smoke that they fell unconscious, while others inhaled such a quantity of snuff that they could not stop sneezing. It was a wonder that Glazunov escaped without injury. The Indians then supplied his party with food and agreed to trade furs with them.

And so went the meeting that was to change the Indians' way of life forever. They offered their services as guides and led the Russians for four winters, concealing the easiest and shortest route to Nulato. From them came sables to grace the shoulders of perfumed Russian counts and their courtesans; a few trinkets bought mink, marten and fox for royalty. With the first Russians came the concept of wealth and poverty; until then the Indians had shared everything. Although the Indians had furs in abundance, steel knives and metal cooking pots were rare. The Russians offered tobacco, tea, snuff, liquor, glass beads, shells, needles, copper, combs, pipes, knives, hatchets, axes and pots. They took Indian women to live with and work for them, and many married them. Some of their children could read, write and swear in Russian. Their offspring became the *coureurs de bois,* true voyageurs of Alaska, the mountain men. Their names still resound along the Yukon: Demoski, Dementieff, Kriska and others.

The boat passed palisades. Captain Art called it the "boneyard," a place below Tanana with sand cliffs about a hundred feet high. The river abraded the rocky schists, which were older than life on earth, and exposed falling, stunted trees. It eroded the debris of peat bogs, the remnants of Pleistocene graves of rhinoceroses and giant ground sloths and mastodon skeletons. Archaeologists dug here looking for fossil remains. The Yukon carried the slow wreckage of the earth down to the sea. The sand was black, shaped in ancient forms, a strange, weird place.

"I can smell rot on a hot day coming through this channel." Art wrinkled his nose. "Don't dare to come too close. The cliff is falling down." What an unsolved mystery this was.

We passed Kallands, thirty-two miles from Tanana, the scene of old mining claims. "We brought mining equipment, built ten miles of road and went broke," says Art. I could see old cabins on shore with tin roofs, deserted now.

It reminded me of the time we went broke gold mining at Rampart in 1950. My husband had the gold fever then, as did many others.

Dave Walker took over the wheel from Captain Art. He set down a large cup of coffee and lit a cigarette. As he turned the wheel he pointed out an old Indian fishwheel to me and the cut cottonwood limbs along the banks which indicated the presence of beaver. The riverbank's eroded soil gave way to open patches of lichen, moss and tundra sedges. Flocks of geese flew overhead and the boat breathed laboriously in low water.

"This whole place used to be caribou country," said Dave. "The first moose came here about the same time as the white man did. The people had to kill, catch or find everything they ate or used. Their clothes were made of tanned skins. They lived in caribou skins and slept under rabbit-skin blankets. The women knew how to make a single long strip of rabbit skin and twine it into a warm blanket.

"They lived in small houses made of logs, moss and mud. Sometimes two shelters of brush and boughs faced each other and families shared a fire between them." Dave piloted three bargeloads skillfully to avoid damage to the propellers. "People didn't stay long in one place. In the upper Tanana they used to lash logs together with spruce root and put flat roofs of poles chinked with moss or spruce bark."

They traveled constantly, walking or using birch-bark canoes, moving in small groups, following the caribou in the winter and fish in the summer. Their trips might take several years, since they traveled to trade, to visit, to hunt and to make war. It was a snowshoe-and-toboggan society.

It was a foggy, dewy, wet, drippy, dead-quiet day on the river, not a soul or living animal in sight. "Some days on the river are like that," Dave said hoarsely.

"Not even a muskrat," I mourned. "Not even a bird in sight. What kind of wilderness is this? Last bird I saw was a gull flying around the salmon racks at a Tanana fish camp. Must be the loud motors scaring everything away."

"It is frightening to come out on the riverbank if you are not accustomed to it," wrote explorer Zagoskin. "There are bear tracks everywhere and beaten trails made by the bears who swim over to the islands to chase moulting birds and fish."

Just when I had given up, Dave spotted a young bull moose on shore, and a few yards away a black bear. We watched as the bear ambled clumsily down the beach and the moose stalked off into the brush in the opposite direction.

"I kill any bear I get a chance to," said Dave. "They'll kill young moose.

"We're coming into Kokrines now, three miles away," he said. "There used to be a large fish camp here. My brother and I freighted ten thousand tons of cargo to Nulato one year for an oil exploration company. As far as we know, nothing developed from it in those days."

The Yukon was a never-ending maze of water patterned with lakes, interlaced with islands and sloughs, a nesting place for waterfowl as well as a paradise for duck hunters.

Indian hunters were well acquainted with the complicated patterns of innumerable lakes. When the water was high, they went from one lake to another through connecting streams.

Flocks of ducks, swans and geese floated on the lakes, concealed by brush and high grasses along the shores. It used to be that when the lucky duck hunter returned home, his wife did all the plucking, and when there was an abundance of ducks, they would have a potlatch, inviting other villagers to come. Their wives kept a good fire going and cooked pot after pot of ducks.

The boat decks were wet with rain, the mountains shrouded in fog. Only the dark spruce was visible, like baleen fringe in a whale's mouth. The changing river was like molten lead, the channels full of snags. Ray, the engineer, and I had the last cup of coffee. "Sure looks like snow is coming soon this year," he repeated.

Many winters along Alaskan rivers have come and gone in my life, and my nostrils have often quivered from the bitter-cold inhalation of sixty-below-zero air.

The forest and tundra were crisscrossed with winter tracks of rabbits, squirrels, ermines, muskrats and foxes. Once we could see the tracks of running caribou or moose and pursuing wolves across the open places. Now the animals have retreated deeper into the wilderness or have been killed in the onslaught of hunters.

The mythic raven alone seemed unperturbed, lording it over us from his vantage point, scavenging. No one ate that black cawing form; he was always treated with awe.

After a long winter came the spring thaw and breakup in the north. On the Yukon, constant streams of broken ice would grind, crash and surge, carrying all before them. The rising river, swollen with whole trees, would tear at the banks, sometimes destroying cabins. Honeycombed ice struck against the crystalline edge of shore ice and exploded into fragments, sounding like smashing glass. Blue sky would finally be reflected in the Yukon, the banks freed of ice, and frogs would announce the arrival of spring.

Every drop of snow then began to drip, splash and trickle, descending into brooks, pools, ponds, plummeting from streams to become meandering rivers. The Yukon flowed on its long journey to the Arctic Circle, reaching salt water in the slate-gray Bering Sea near Siberia.

Then, as if by magic, deep snows lying in the wilderness forest disappeared to reveal violet crocuses. The first green leaves appeared on the scrub willows and the white birches, and the songs of the birds were heard in the northern forests.

For me it was a time of rejuvenation; my breathing became easier with the rivers flowing freely, with the lifting of the winter ice shroud and the rebirth of the land.

Years ago I had read of a prospector bicycling down the Yukon. I could visualize him bundled in furs on his bike, peddling the icy, perilous paths from village to village in forty below zero. I went to sleep dreaming of the eerie sensation I had felt driving our car over the frozen river at fifty below zero in Fairbanks, then imagining I was the lone bike rider on a white, silent Yukon, pedaling with hot, steamy breath floating behind me. I awoke from my dream just as I was about to fall into a wide ice crack. I heard the boat engine giving off a steady, familiar pulse, like the beating of a heart, and I sighed in relief, turning over in my sleep.

CHAPTER 7

Nuchalawoya

In a state of nature, once a year, without their women, they descended on Tanana in birch canoes, in full accoutrement of pointed coats, beads, feathers and ochered hair . . . No white man had penetrated the wilds in which they pursued the caribou and trapped the fox and sable. Their reserve, fierce demeanor and the mystery which surrounded their manner of life had its effect on the imagination of the adjacent tribes, who seemed to fear them.

WILLIAM H. DALL, *1898*

I've been left from your grandmothers
And grandfathers, your aunts and uncles.
In my time, us native people,
Long before you were born,
We don't worry about the money
We don't worry about the grant
We worry about the hunt
We worry about the trap
We worry about the moose
We worry about the cold
And how we are going to make it.

CHIEF ANDREW ISAAC,
traditional chief of Tanacross, 1977

TANANA, located in the middle of Athabaskan country, is the trading center. In June 1964 I had visited Tanana to attend the traditional festival called the Nuchalawoya, meaning "the place where two rivers meet." (*Nuchalawoya* is originated in antiquity, long before the discovery of America.) At the festival there was an important gathering of the Tanana chiefs to discuss the survival of Indian life and culture. At the summer solstice they met to resolve problems and to divide up the hunting grounds so that everyone would have enough to eat.

The chiefs were distinguished not by moose hide and dentalium; they wore white man's clothing. Among them were Chief Peter John; Chief Andrew Isaac; Ralph Perdue, president of the Fairbanks Native Association; Alfred Ketzler, president of the Nenana group, and other Indians from other villages.

At the Nuchalawoya the Minto villagers were first to arrive, signaling their coming with three gunshots late at night and with eight boats lashed together in the traditional way. (Before motorboats were used, guests paddled birch-bark canoes and chanted in unison, passing over the water as swiftly as a flock of ducks.) Everyone then sang and laughed and discharged shots into the air. The Tanana Indians sang their welcome song from the banks while an old man greeted them in Athabaskan.

Every family took in relatives and friends from other villages. I was lucky to find sleeping space with the Clevelands, the Episcopal minister and his wife. I shared a single bed with an Eskimo girl from Fairbanks. Mrs. Cleveland, a capable, hard-working woman, made us breakfast in a huge skillet, breaking twelve eggs without bursting a single yolk. I thought that quite a feat, since I had trouble with two. The Reverend Tom Cleveland, a grandson of President Cleveland, had brought his large family to Tanana. They were all athletic and reminded me of the Kennedys. (I found out later that they were friends.)

Canoes raced across the Yukon while the villagers on the bank shouted for their favorites. A greased-pole–walking contest was next, and one contestant after another fell off into the icy Yukon as each lost his balance. Finally one Indian boy made it by running across with sure bare feet.

Contests and games included jumps, foot races, bow-and-arrow contests, three-legged races, obstacle runs around barrels and under beams, marathon motorboat races and a tea-making race—contestants had to find wood, build a fire and, after making the tea, rush back across the river. Tom Cleveland won the arm-wrestling contest against the villagers.

In the community hall the women cooked all day. Three men split and sawed wood to keep the open fire going under the big pot of moose-head soup. In addition to the soup there were ducks, fish, jello, bread, wild rhubarb, pilot bread and tea.

In 1962, twenty-eight Indian representatives had met in Tanana to form the Tanana Chiefs Conference. Three white people were instrumental: Charley Purvis, his daughter DeLois Ketzler (wife of Alfred Ketzler) and Kay Hitchcock. (Kay, who had been an art student of mine at the University of Alaska, had written a dissertation on the Alaskan land claims.) Before 1962, there had been no Indian organization except the Alaska Native Brotherhood, formed in 1912 by Indians of southern Alaska. But in 1962 the Indians were worried about the land because government surveyors were scouting villages and staking claims in and around the village sites.

Alfred Ketzler was the first president elected. Ketzler later met with the southeastern Indians and the Eskimos, helping to unify Alaskan natives. Many other young Indian leaders, such as Emil Notti, John Sackett, Richard Frank, Jimmy Huntington, Sam Kito, Maurice Thompson, Mitch Demientieff and Tim Wallis, also fought for their land. Among the younger Alaskan women, Mary Jane Fate, Georgiana Lincoln, Ruby Tansy John and Lucy Carlo have been prominent leaders. Mary Jane served as national president of the North American Indian Women's Association.

Father Convert, priest at Nulato, was asked to represent Kaltag, Nulato and Holy Cross, all Catholic villages. Alfred Grant represented Tanana, Ralph Perdue and Nick Gray came from Fairbanks, and Kay Hitchcock was appointed acting secretary. Charley Purvis and his daughter were observers, as were many politicians, including Senator Ernest Gruening, for it was an election year.

In the days that followed, the Indians prepared a statement of their views and problems, welding themselves into a unit, speaking with one voice, calling themselves Dena Nena Henash ("Our Land Speaks"). They said they no longer had any way to feed their children except to live on relief and they would not allow this destruction of themselves and their children. "Our people always thought they owned the land where they lived and hunted. We did not lose it by war and we did not sell it. We still feel it is ours. But we find that no one, the State included, thinks we have a right to our homes or the land where we hunt and fish, although the United States did recognize it. The State is invading and selling our land. There are no jobs in the villages and our hunting grounds are being taken away."

In the cool of the evening, the Minto dancers were led by Peter Jimmie, carrying his feathered stick, dressed in beaded moose-skin headband and moccasins. The women wore long fringed dresses embellished with beads and feathers.

Especially impressive was the regional leader Chief Andrew Isaac, traditional chief from Tanacross, "Keeper of the Old Legends and Clan Lines," born in 1898. His small group of dancers, older men and women, moved with solemnity and dignity.

The Bureau of Land Management once notified him that his land allotment (160 acres, allowed each Indian under federal law) was cut because the agency felt "that the owner was not making sufficient use of the land." When white men came to inspect the land, they saw nothing disturbed, fields unplowed, hills not bulldozed, for Indians hunted on the land and left it as it was.

In 1964, after the chiefs' meeting, Chief Isaac filed a blanket claim to prevent the state of Alaska from selling vacant lots on George Lake, the Crow band's ancestral lands, at the New York World's Fair, as a tourist gimmick. The state Division of Lands employee who defended the Indian rights to this land was fired, but the sale was stopped.

Chief Isaac said during the land claims: "We are slowly being squeezed to death. No one has ever come out and talked to us to see what we think or how we feel [about] what is going on. We are not a chess game. We are human beings and are right now very upset and disturbed. We feel our land and what it has grown has fed and clothed and helped us survive. Do you wonder why we are fighting to keep it?"

Chief Isaac and Chief Peter John understood early that the land was the most important thing. "If they would just give me the title to land that we owned, I'd forget the money," said Chief Isaac. "I never went to school a day in my life, but I know that at the age of ten I started to wear cloth instead of skin clothing and I've never been warm enough since.

"My people have lived off the land through the ages. When we killed an animal we used every bit of it, making clothing and tools with what we didn't eat."

William Paul, Tlingit Indian lawyer, had for years spearheaded a drive to organize Athabaskan Indians into the Alaska Native Brotherhood, but few had been interested except the southeastern Alaskan Indians. I remember meeting William Paul in the fifties at his sister's house in Fairbanks. He was frustrated about the Indians' lack of interest. Paul lived to see the land claims settlement ten years later and helped to formulate the legal terms.

The Alaska Native Claims Settlement Act set up twelve regional corporations of Alaska. Each villager was now a stockholder receiving one hundred shares in a corporation. Doyon, one of the Indian profit-making corporations, has assets equal to General Motors.

On the second day of the Nuchalawoya, an abundance of moose stew was served to everyone. The Tanana women bustled about serving homemade bread, pilot crackers, jello, coffee and tea. Many took sugar in their tea, but Chief Isaac remembered his first taste of sugar in 1907. "It was so terrible I spit it out and wiped my mouth up and down my sleeve to get rid of every bit of it."

We all sat on benches along the wall in the community house and watched the dancers until late. Children and teenagers danced to a frenetic drumbeat, singing the old songs. Mrs. Jimmie of Minto, one of the lead dancers, motioned me to come up and dance in the circle with them, but I was too shy, although I wanted to dance very much.

After midnight two guitarists took over with country music and the younger set prevailed.

The white population of Tanana included nurses and doctors from the Tanana Hospital, pilots, construction workers and teachers.

While they watched the contestants of the various competitions in the sunshine, I walked along the riverfront and noticed that the cabins were mostly ramshackle log houses, the church being the most imposing structure.

One cabin looked just like the rest except that in the window wild roses and bluebells grew in a Hills Brothers coffee can. It began to rain and Margaret Kokrine, whose home it was, invited me to come in and dry off.

Inside, the cabin had a flavor of past Tanana history, a blending of Indian and white cultures resembling the flavor of cabins I had seen in backwoods mining communities. The barrel stove with the woodpile behind it was the focal center of the room, with several black-spider frying pans hanging over it. The washbasin in the corner had cupboards over it, holding a display of cups, plates, kettles and a teapot. A white cat slept on the rocking chair.

To the right was a room with a huge, high four-poster bed. A bathtub in one corner of it was filled with cartons of books and old photographs. On the wall was a Charles Russell print of an Indian shooting buffalo, which Margaret's husband, Gregory, had won in a raffle. There were two carved wooden chairs and an antique chest of drawers with a marble top.

Gregory, an Apache Indian, chopped their wood and took care of their needs. Their house was called "the pan house" because it was the center for the gambling game of pan.

Over sixty and arthritic, Margaret had high cheekbones and blue eyes. Old photographs of her grandmother showed a woman in a fur parka trimmed with fur tails and decorated with intricate geometric black-and-white designs; her boots were made of caribou legs. Another woman in the photo had chin tattoos, made by rubbing sinew in charcoal, then inserting it through the skin.

The men in the photos wore moose or caribou skins with the hair inside, the traditional shirt reaching to mid-thigh and ending in a point front and back. Large gauntlet mittens were hung from straps over their shoulders, and marten fur caps covered their heads.

One of the photographs showed Indian women parading the latest fashion of leg-o'-mutton sleeves; other women and their children were dressed with clothes from a missionary's barrel.

When the photographs had been taken, there were three thousand people in Tanana. The village had a wooden boardwalk, a grocery, a lodge, a telephone station and a cavalry post, Fort Gibbon. Mail was carried by horse sled in winter and by boat in the summer. White people lived in two-story frame houses with big gardens full of vegetables and flowers. The first vegetable ever planted there was turnips. According to Margaret, "There was even a Chinese restaurant and laundry. The main income in the village was from whiskey and wood."

Four burly miners sporting handlebar mustaches were photographed drinking beer. Some of the miners in the area had married Indian women and settled there, but many had raped and run, leaving pregnant Indian girls.

During the gold rush of the early 1900's, there were many dances at the mission. The trappers and miners would come to town on December 22 and dance until ten days after New Year's. The festivities ended with the Trapper's Ball, in which everyone danced to the tunes of violins, banjos and guitars.

I painted the little girl standing by the blue kitchen door near the stove and woodpile. I seemed to have a fascination for people near woodpiles and stoves, perhaps because cabin life centered around it.

Overheard at Tanana: "We look down on the upper Yukon River Indians because they speak a different dialect. We feel we are higher-class Indians."

A story told of an old man: "He had ordered a wife from the Sears Roebuck catalog. He figured if that fat book had all those models and more merchandise than he ever imagined existed, why couldn't they find him a wife? He never did get a wife, even though he waited a long time, but he did get a bundle of clothes."

I had seen Grandma Maggie Short, a tiny white-haired woman, at the Indian dances. Although wrinkled, she had the sweetness of the very young. She did not know the exact date of her birth, but it was said that she was over one hundred years old and had seen the first steamboat come down the river.

Officially she was called Mrs. Elia, her husband's name, but when I asked her name, she said, "Maggie Short."

I painted her wearing her dentalium necklace, with the natural light coming in from her window. Her teakettle gave off steam and her wood stove crackled. Her mouth and cheeks lifted upward, no sign of dejection or depression on her face; it was a lively face, and she held the pose for the hour that I painted her.

Grandma reminisced about her youth: "In the springtime we'd go up the river in boats, tie them together. We'd fish all summer on the Yukon—good fish there, oily-skinned salmon, at the rapids. Then we'd make a raft and drift down with the fish. The only time we were short of food was early in the springtime, before the fish come."

Grandma pushed back her white hair and continued: "We used to get the porcupine. Build a fire, burn off his quills, scrape it and boil it. It's good.

"Those days they had no law and all that, 'Don't kill this' and 'Don't do that.' It wasn't like that a long time ago. It was free. Everything was free. And that's the way we used to live."

I was not aware of the passing of time, although several times I asked if she wanted to stop. I thought I was tiring her, but she said no. When I finished the painting, Maggie gasped and said softly, "I'm scared."

I believe she felt, as some of the Eskimo women I had painted, that it was a form of magic to catch her spirit or likeness on canvas, and that it was a supernatural act. I said nothing, hoping that her daughter, who was a nurse, would explain that a painting took nothing away from the model but rather immortalized her.

When Grandma Short was a very young girl, the minister asked all the people to gather and he baptized them, gave them a cross, then married them as they had never been married before. It was their custom to have many wives.

Grandma recalled the reverend saying, " 'You can only have one wife. The first one.' Everyone cried. Only the first wife could he keep and the rest had to go. So many were big and ready to have babies. No one knew who would take care of them.

"The chief was told to let his wives go. He hollered and made a big speech and he said, 'I won't let go my wives,' " recollected Grandma. "And he said to the other men, 'You scared of this fellow, to let go your wives?' They couldn't do nothing with him, just let him go and have his wives."

Fifty-nine canoes filled with Indians, around 450 Indians, were confirmed. At that time, eight medicine men, among them the best known on the Tanana River, stood up before the whole congregation, publicly renounced their former practices and promised they would never make medicine anymore.

The writer William H. Dall wrote in 1898 that "the Indians were fond of singing and tobacco; and for a pipeful you could baptize a whole tribe." However, they still practiced traditional Indian medicine, although they hesitated to tell white people about such events.

The church considered Indians uncivilized pagans. It introduced another set of songs and rituals; it made the Indians ashamed of their own beliefs and discouraged the use of their own language. The Indians had felt preaching was a poor substitute for curing ills, locating game or predicting the future, but gradually the missionaries won their confidence.

Confessions, so important to the missionaries, were of no interest to the old medicine men—they were supposed to know who the people were who had broken taboos. Nor did medicine men consider drinking, swearing and other activities so deplored by missionaries to be their concern.

The powers of the shamans were derided by whites, and the medicine men were driven underground. Some of the shamans had helped cure their people and had worked unselfishly for them, while others had used their powers to cause fear.

The Indians gathered together in Tanana in 1964 without their medicine men, but they had not lost a feeling of unity. The people gathered at this Nuchalawoya had forged themselves into one voice speaking out of the wilderness, a voice that became the beginning of a movement that culminated in the settlement of the Native land claims in Alaska.

The Tanana chiefs have grown from a volunteer staff of two to a large organization covering forty-two villages. Their budget is millions of dollars. They now contract for other agencies, such as the Bureau of Indian Affairs, and care for the villages in areas of health, water, housing, education and welfare. The process is a slow one, but at least now the people have more control over their own destinies.

In spite of new housing and electricity in some villages, many things remain the same. The money from the claims settlement went mainly to the corporations, most of which have yet to declare dividends and some of which have announced losses. However, the Bureau of Indian Affairs boarding schools are being phased out and local high schools are being built. Educational radio and television stations are being built and health care has improved. Michael Krause, distinguished linguist at the University of Alaska Language Center, has struggled to develop village programs requiring bilingual teachers to preserve the languages of the various groups. Health aides communicate with hospitals by radio, often via satellite. When I first went to the villages, almost every family had a case of tuberculosis; now the TB wing of the Anchorage Native Hospital is closed for lack of patients.

The old chieftains who had warred against one another in the past were gone, along with the chiefs who sat for photographs. In their place now sat new chiefs intent on Indian unity because it meant their survival.

CHAPTER 8

Galena

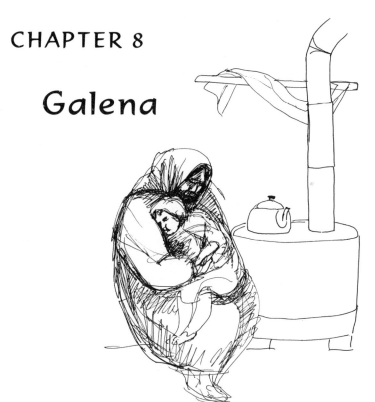

Once upon a time there lived a man in a camp.
He had with him a little child. Each day he'd go out
hunting, and every time he'd come home he'd notice the
child's lips were greasy. One day when the grandpa
came home he said, "Grandson, how come your lips
are greasy?" He said, "My brother puts his lips to
mine. That is what causes that." One day the grandpa
got curious and came home earlier. Here was a wolf in
the house with the child. The grandpa said to the wolf,
"Why don't you stay with us so you will be our dog?"
So it started living with them; it'd kill caribou for them,
and Grandpa always saved the best parts of the caribou
for the wolf, the ribs and fat.
    One day a crow came to them and said to Grandpa,
"Why don't you let me have the wolf for a while?"
Finally the crow talked him into it, but Grandpa told
the crow, "I always feed him the best because he is
the one that feeds us, kills animals for us." So the
crow took the wolf. Later on in the evening Grandpa
heard the wolf crying, saying, "Why did you give me
away?" The grandpa started up the next day. He came
to a place where the wolf had killed a caribou. The
crow was eating away, the best parts. He didn't even
bother to clean the guts. Those he gave to the wolf.
The wolf kept eating the guts that were not cleaned.
That is the reason for the wolf to have yellowish feet
and nose.

JENNIE HUNTINGTON, *"Wolf Story,"* Galena.
Translated by Poldine Carlo, Alaska Library Project

WE docked at Galena on an overcast, chilly day. I had slept through the stop at the village of Ruby. I walked down the narrow plank from the boat to a dirt trail which had been widened to permit cars to drive the ten miles of waterfront roads. I was the only one getting off the barge.

Galena was named by white men who discovered galena, a lead ore, there in 1918. It began as a village called Natulaten, but gradually the white man's influence made itself felt, and eventually an army base was installed, bringing in trucks, cars and planes and a money-based economy. The town was considered strategic because its airfield could accommodate jet planes. Jobs were created by the military installations and tracking stations.

Galena was full of junked, defunct machinery, which lay derelict everywhere, cancer sores of the twentieth century. Old deserted trucks and their innards were strewn as if in the aftermath of battle. A rusty car without wheels lay full of bullet holes oozing filth.

A raw wind cut through my sweater as I walked along, carrying my oil box. Rickety stovepipes leaned tipsily from plywood shacks, crowded together. Fish were pinned to a line with clothespins! A tin bathtub hung from the side of a house. Numerous outhouses testified to the fact that there was no running water or plumbing. An Indian woman passed me, her head wrapped in bandages.

A girl leaned out her shack window and gave me a sour look as I shifted my paint box. WINE, BEER, AND WILD, WILD WOMEN read the printed sign along the road. A middle-aged woman with a black eye and a man staggering after her came out of Hobo's Bar at ten in the morning.

Garbage lined the entranceway of Hobo's Bar, the only lodge for two hundred miles. It had nine rooms plus a dining room, bar and poolroom. The walls were covered with faded paintings entitled "Shooting of Dan McGrew," painted by an artist from Seattle who had tended bar, cooked for three years and painted her customers into the mural.

Hobo's was rough, but it was warm and dry, the roof did not leak and you could get a meal, a drink and a place to sleep.

Another sign read:

WHEN THE WHITE MAN DISCOVERED THIS COUNTRY,
THE INDIANS WERE RUNNING IT.
THERE WERE NO TAXES, NO DEBTS,
THE WOMAN DID ALL THE WORK,
AND THE WHITE MAN THOUGHT HE COULD IMPROVE
ON A SYSTEM LIKE THAT!

The decrepit building, used to hard knocks, almost burned down several times from electrical shorts and explosions, and once a tar pot caught on fire. It is said that during the flood, Hobo put a chair up to the bar top and sat there with a drink, daring the fates to dislodge him. It took seven feet of Yukon water and a friend in scuba gear to get him out.

Guns have been fired in Hobo's Bar, but only four people have actually been shot and only one has died, which is some kind of Alaskan record. Hobo himself was shot by a woman looking for her husband, who had run into the back room. The bullet came through the door, hitting Hobo under one eye, but he survived. One man was shot and killed while he sat with someone else's wife.

When the phone took one Galena man's last dime, he did what many of us have been tempted to do but have never had the nerve to. He came back with a twelve-gauge shotgun and put the phone out of commission. Its mechanical arteries, looking like a modern sculpture, still testified to its disintegration. The sign nearby read, YE PUBLIC TELEPHONE.

I talked to an old Indian in a checked shirt drinking at the bar. "When I was young," he said, "I didn't have this kind of shirt. I used buckskin summer caribou pants and a marten fur robe to sleep on and a coat of rabbit skin. Can't freeze with that in sixty below. It took a long time to start a fire, no matches! But we didn't freeze.

"When the white men discovered this country, the womenfolks were doing all the work. They brought the White Mule and showed us how to make it, then they threw us in jail for drinking it.

"Them days, the womenfolks hauled dry willows for wood. No axes. Cook, wash dishes, diapers, skin whatever animals we brought home. All the man had to do was hunt, trap, make fishtraps, snowshoes, sleds, birch-bark canoes.

"White people we didn't know came to this country. They tried to trap, only they got no meat. We gave them meat. He got nothing to eat; we feed him. What we got we helped them with. Never let them starve." He drank his beer and wiped his mouth with the back of his big hand. "Indian people should charge the license for white people to hunt instead of them charging us.

"Sometimes it takes us over a week to get a moose. Then we have to skin it, haul it in by dogs. That's work. One year it was seventy below zero. Thirty miles out I shot a moose. I had to build a big fire, lost two dogs, my knife just froze." He stopped for a beer.

"We sell Alaska for seven million dollars. What Indian get out of that? He didn't get nothing. All he gets is a little relief. Pension. Food stamps and hospital. The hospital we go to when we get the disease white man brought us. White people, he think Indians just like a dog. He didn't care. We didn't treat white people like that when they first come here."

Another old Indian who had been sitting at the end of the bar turned to answer: "Maybe you're right, but tell me, did you ever have to starve before white man came? Did you ever have to eat rabbit shit?"

We all fell silent then. What was the answer? It seemed to me that I could look around and find children still half-starving right in the villages.

Still lugging my heavy paint box, I walked aimlessly on the dirt road that was Galena's main street. Offshoots of cabins meandered without thought or plan, for Galena had grown like Topsy.

I entered a small grocery store that sold starches, ten kinds of beans and an array of potato chips, gravy mixes in packages, marshmallow cream, candy, Coke and sweet punch—the dentist's friends, all poor people's fill-up food.

Prices were twice as high as those in Fairbanks, which until then I thought had the highest prices in the nation. With the decline of subsistence hunting and without means of making money, some people faced a daily crisis just to survive. This typical village store sold food that lacked basic nutrients; it is hoped that the people subsisted on moose or fish. However, this grocer had a sense of humor. The rack of paperback books included a copy of *Do You Sincerely Want to Be Rich?*

I asked a woman in the store who would be a good model to paint, and was directed to Bessie Wholecheese's house. Her sprawling log cabin had a front porch stacked with dried fish and miscellaneous tools. A large husky nursing three pups blocked the entranceway. I smelled wood smoke and salmon.

I stepped over the pups and greeted Bessie, who invited me in. A pleasant, rounded woman with a strong face and long gray hair, she gave the impression of great inner strength. Geranium plants grew on her windowsill, and her huge room was warmed by a homemade barrel

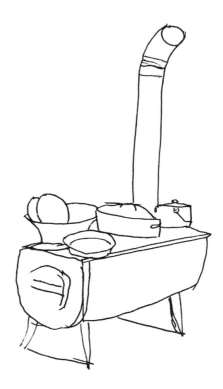

stove, topped with a large teakettle and a five-gallon water can. Her daughter sat rocking her newborn baby beneath a black-velvet wall hanging of Jesus.

I told Bessie that I was traveling on the boat and would like to paint her, offering to pay for her time.

"What, pay me for sitting still?" she laughed.

After we chatted about the boat, the weather and her family, Bessie sat placidly near her stove. I placed my oil box on a chair and sat on another one facing her. Drying socks hung on the line over the stove, and I heard the faint sizzle of rain splattering against a hot chimney pipe. The warm hearth and cozy stillness of her house appealed to me after the noisy boat. Bessie's tranquility and cheerfulness and her solid personality were nourishing for me. She was as she seemed to be. It began to rain harder outside, slapping the window with drops, and the teakettle made a gurgling sound on the hot stove. Her latest grandchild slept peacefully.

I painted her curved forms, her full womanly breasts, with her arms folded over her round belly, her sleeves rolled up over her strong forearms. Her shapes contrasted with those of the stove, somehow tied to its symmetry—the woman and the hearth, tied symbolically.

Bessie had given birth to twenty-two children, of which eight had died. At fifty-nine, she had twenty-six grandchildren. There was not a wrinkle on her face. All but the last three children had been born in her home with the help of whoever happened to be present. "Once there was a girl here and I told her what to do," she said casually. "I never had no trouble." And yet eight had died, probably of tuberculosis or at childbirth.

We established an easy rapport. She appreciated the fact that I was a countrywoman, an Alaskan used to the woods, not a tourist but one who had weathered many northern winters and who understood village life.

In contrast to Bessie's home deliveries, her daughter had her baby in the Anchorage Hospital and was in labor twenty-two hours. She did not breast-feed her baby, as Bessie had, but gave him a modern plastic nipple to suck.

Bessie did not have much use for doctors. "Nowadays if a girl has a little pain, she runs to the doctor," she said. She believed in her own natural health and in her ability to take care of herself. She ate simply and worked hard, fishing in the summer and through the ice in the winter, chopping wood and usually shooting her own moose.

In Bessie's grandmother's time, Indians were considered married when the man moved in and helped the girl's family to hunt. Bessie and Edgar Nollner lived together following the Indian tradition. Edgar, descended from one of the first settlers of Galena, was one of the dog mushers who rushed the diphtheria serum to Nome in the winter of 1925.

Together they had filled a big freezer with moose and fish. A practical man, Edgar had built four rafts and a house on oil drums just in case the water threatened to flood again.

When I left I thanked her and put some money where Bessie would find it later. The painting had strength and I liked it; I would finish it at home in my studio. I liked the title, too—"Bessie Wholecheese of Galena."

I was invited to visit a young couple who had just inherited a house and truck. The young father was hooking up a new oil stove, muttering, "It's a lot of work cutting wood when the snow is deep." He did not have a job at present, and a drum of oil was expensive.

His tiny wife, only seventeen, was heating water over the two-burner stove to give their baby a bath. "She's had a cold all month. This is the first time I've had a chance to bathe her."

I helped her bathe the baby in a white basin similar to the one I had used. The baby was a beauty, but I could feel her lung congestion when I lifted her. The mother dressed and wrapped her in a warm blanket and then put her to sleep in the crib with a bottle.

I wondered why the trend in the villages was not to nurse babies when white women were making efforts to nurse. The Catholic churches on the Yukon encouraged nursing but did not condone birth control.

The couple had a good start compared to most young people, since they owned a house, truck, new stove, sewing machine, couch and rug, and except for running water and a job, they were comfortable. They offered me coffee and I shared the canned fruit I had purchased at the store. The mother drank Coca-cola incessantly, although it made her stomach hurt.

After Galena was flooded with thirteen feet of water and damaged by blocks of ice larger than the houses, Jimmy Huntington and John Sackett, both prominent Indian leaders, had helped to rehabilitate the village. They had helped transform another village, Huslia, from a derelict fish camp to a model community. Huntington, a trader and dog musher, told his fascinating life story in his book, *On the Edge of Nowhere*. He later served in the Alaska State House of Representatives. Sackett, at the age of twenty-two in 1967 the youngest member ever to be elected, also served in the House. He was now the head of the Finance Committee, a powerful figure in the Alaskan legislature.

Federal housing dollars were to build thirty new homes with sewers and running water a mile from the village on Alexander Lake. Set back from the Yukon, they would be safe from flooding.

The ten miles of road in Galena were a disaster for one man who drove his car off into the mighty Yukon!

When I walked down the street, a man ran after me, asking if I was the welfare lady.

"No," I replied, "I'm the artist lady."

It was raining and the wind was cutting. I put on my eighty-five-cent monkey-face gloves that I had purchased in the store and carried my heavy oil box to the boat, holding tight to the new portrait of Bessie that waved in the wind.

CHAPTER 9

Ella Vernetti
of Koyukuk

*The old crow was a medicine man. He was paddling down
the Yukon. He had heard that further down the river was a
very young girl whose father was a rich man. Before he got
to their camp, he landed and picked some moss, which he
put on himself. He closed his eyes. When he opened his eyes,
he had a beautiful pair of boots made of wolverine skin. He
kept picking different leaves and roots, rubbing them on
himself and closing his eyes. When he opened his eyes, he'd
have a parka, mittens, just everything at all fancy. So he
started down the river in his canoe. He landed and went up
to the house. In the house the young woman gave him a
dish of food. The people said the chief from up the river had
come that night. The crow was saying to himself, "I wish that
young girl would go to sleep." So she did. With that he took
her out in her sleep and put her in his canoe and took off
down the river. Soon they came to a place where they had
to spend the night. He said to himself, "I wish she would
wake up." Soon after, she woke up, and what she saw was a
crow. All the nice clothes had disappeared. She started
to cry, but he already had her; there was no turning back.*

FABIAN GEORGE,
"Koyukon legend."
*Translated by Poldine Carlo and
Liza Jones, Alaska Library Project*

THE bright full moon yellowed up the Yukon, shining directly into my window. The pungent gamy scent of highbush cranberries and bog blueberries floated up from the woods.

Three long blasts warned of our boat's arrival at the small village of Koyukuk after midnight. Children were jumping up and down. Long-haired teenagers with headbands and jeans, hands in pockets, strolled along the waterfront. There were no streetlights, no electricity. A few kerosene lamps flickered on in the cabins as we pulled closer. Dogs growled.

"It's like Indian villages used to be fifty years ago," Captain Art said as he supervised the unloading operations.

The Ella and Dominic Vernetti Trading Post is synonymous with Koyukuk's history, its name known the length of the Yukon. Each year as the Yukon rose and flooded the village, the Vernettis would put their groceries on the top shelves of the store and move into the second story until the flood was over. I often saw them at the Old Nordale Hotel in Fairbanks before it burned down. Ella, a graceful woman with proud carriage, had worn her gray hair in a topknot. I saw Dominic briefly before he died, a heavyset, bald Italian suffering from diabetes. Their children were educated and lived in the States, except for Mary, who helped to run the store.

The river slowly ate away at the bank in front of the Vernettis' trading post. Where once two wagons could pass, there was now only a foot trail. The fifteen families who lived in Koyukuk could still take long dog-sled rides to the next village or faster rides by plane or motorboat.

The boat pulled up in front of the trading post in the dark of the night while the men unloaded with a fork lift, piling the groceries and supplies in front of the warehouse. Ella's daughter Mary supervised the unloading.

"It's a small dying village," said the captain from the pilothouse. "They were dependent upon Ella. When the other villages ran out of food and came to her, she saved it for her people at Koyukuk. She taught the women to make doll clothes for extra income and she sold the kids a limit of Coke so their teeth wouldn't rot."

Everyone came to her with his or her problems. Ella had also been the village nurse, delivering babies, pulling teeth and attending to every minor or major illness or accident.

"There is no industry at all here except fire fighting," said the captain, shifting his weight as he sat down. "One thing, in this village they don't use oil stoves, they cut wood. It's cheaper."

The men of Koyukuk hunted and cut wood at the same time. After cutting logs, they made a raft to float downriver. In town they piled the wood on the bank and used it all winter to keep the houses warm.

Dominic had come from Italy to work for his uncle, who gold-mined on Vault Creek. He followed the gold stampede to Ruby, struck it rich on the Hog River, a tributary of the Koyukuk, and started a trading post with the profits. Later a rich vein of gold was found in the exact spot he had pitched his tent, with an even larger mother lode under his outhouse. Sometimes he was sorry he had not stuck to mining instead of trading, but in 1924 he sold his trading post and started another at Koyukuk, where the sternwheelers unloaded cargo into shallower scows for trips to Bettles and Wiseman.

Ella was born in Chena, six miles from Fairbanks, to sternwheeler Captain William Blair and the Athabaskan woman who was his housekeeper and cook. When the captain's wife arrived from the States, she insisted that the captain finance Ella's education.

Her grade-school days with her grandmother in the mining tent city of Ruby were a traumatic experience for Ella. She was the only Indian child in a white school where Indians were not allowed. She once said she learned while she was young that unless she stood up for her own rights, no one else would.

After high school Ella headed for Koyukuk to teach school for one year, then to the University of Washington. Back in Koyukuk in 1925, she stoked the big barrel stove in the one-room schoolhouse with four-foot chunks of wood and pumped the big gas-powered lights to make the room bright enough for reading. She cared for the young children as if they were her own, and her zeal communicated itself to them. Children from simple homes barely able to read were taught ballet and art in addition to the basics of reading and writing.

Ella had planned to stay one more year, but she married Dominic Vernetti and made Koyukuk her home. Their store sold large bolts of calico and flannel, reindeer meat, canned stuffs and sealskin mukluks made by the Eskimos at Unalakleet. Business was so good that they opened up three more stores, at Dalby, Hog River and Huslia.

The store never handled pennies or small change, but traded furs for groceries. They were given credit with wooden coins, called bingles.

The Vernettis appraised the skins the Indians trapped before sending them to the Seattle fur market, for their livelihood depended on the fur trade. Ella encouraged the women to make crafts for sale, and sold them to the Fairbanks stores.

Ella had a heart attack while cleaning fish along the Yukon. She died in heart surgery in a California hospital far from home.

Two years later, Ella's family gathered enough gifts and food to honor her with a stick dance. The stick dance, or Feast of the Dead, is a variation of the potlatch, a time for people to repay any help they received at the time of death of a beloved relative or family member. A long pole with ribbons and feathers and two rust-colored sticks called clappers were prepared. The women once wore a headdress resembling caribou horns, but now they wore feathered headbands.

The week-long ceremony was an important ritual which honored the deceased and hastened the reincarnation of their souls. It provided an emotional release for the bereaved villagers and their guests. There was much feasting every night and singing and dancing. A special song was made up for the deceased. Men sat on a bench and sang thirteen old songs that were sung only on this night. Women in feathered headdresses and colorful clothes lined up in front of the singers and danced, moving only their arms and the middle parts of their bodies in rhythm.

During the dances in the evening, a loud knocking announced the men who entered carrying the stick pole, a fifteen-foot stripped spruce pole decorated with ribbons and feathers. The men lashed the pole upright to a crossbeam in the skylight, and then men and women danced clockwise around the pole, singing. The people danced and sang surging around the pole all night long. Blankets, material, gloves and other gifts were piled in a corner, and mink, beaver, wolf and marten pelts were tied to the stick. Eventually the stick pole was taken out of the hall, and people sang and danced with it all over town. Finally they took the pole, broke it and scattered the pieces across the frozen Yukon.

The most important part of the ceremony was the "dressing," which took place the evening after the stick dance. Behind a curtain the selected people received clothes. Then they appeared in the new clothes, including beautiful new fur parkas and beaded moccasins, and left the hall without looking back, for it would bring bad luck. They represented dead people, and many women cried, I was told, recalling their loved ones. The gifts, including the furs, were then distributed to the people who had helped the deceased. The next day the people representing the dead walked around the village and shook hands with the villagers, saying the final good-bys.

I wished I could have been there, but I gathered what had happened from other people's accounts. People came from villages scattered up and down the Yukon and other places to attend Ella's stick dance. A few years ago two women from another village traveled on snowshoes with babies on their backs to attend a stick dance. It was a time for getting rid of grief, a reenactment of old beliefs in reincarnation, which some priests had tried unsuccessfully to eradicate.

At Koyukuk, Ella Vernetti, rejected by white people as a child, had lived her life in service to the people of her mother's blood. In the end, it was they who honored her.

CHAPTER 10

Nulato

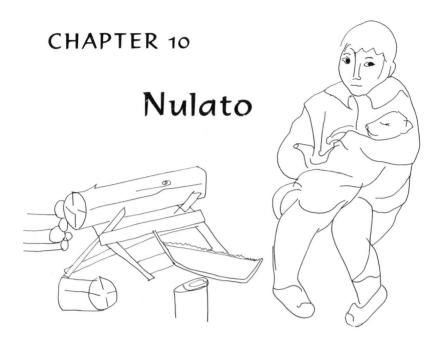

A group of Indians encircled the invalid; in their
midst burnt a dim fire. A monotonous chorus in an
undertone was kept up . . . [The shaman] appeared
to draw the evil spirit from the sick man and,
wrestling with it, threw it on the fire and then
repelled, ran wildly from it with mock terror. . . .
Now it has possession of him, and he gesticulated,
groaned and frothed at the mouth, the whole
accompanied . . . by the chorus. The whole
affair was a weird scene in . . . overhanging trees,
the twilight, the low fire.
    At last the performance assumed a gayer tinge,
the chorus grew louder and livelier; the man was
supposed to be dispossessed, and he hobbled
from the scene.

FREDERICK WHYMPER, *1869*

THE village of Nulato lay spread
out in the dull, drizzly morning rain. Indians sat on tree stumps watching the freight being unloaded from the boat. The only other movements were those of the usual roaming mongrels sniffing the banks. The cemetery overlooking the village marked Nulato as one of the most picturesque on the Yukon. Its history was the bloodiest because of the Nulato massacre.

In 1841, Vasily Derabin was sent by Russia to Nulato to rebuild the fort which the Indians had twice burned down, giving presents to the most influential chiefs. He built a settlement consisting of several log houses, without a stockade or adequate means of defense; obviously the Russians wanted to impress on the Indians that they had come peacefully.

The Indians Derabin met were well-fed hunters and warriors; game was plentiful. Dressed in double-tailed coats, they wore trousers that were a combination of pants and moccasins. Their hair was daubed in vermilion clay and dusted with eagle down. Frederick Whymper, an artist who visited Nulato, saw the red clay on the Indians' hair, supposed that they had some terrible head disease and offered soap. An Indian took the soap and smiled at Whymper's ignorance of fashion.

The Russians bartered glass beads, needles, knives, hatchets, earrings, cloth, copper kettles, mirrors and tobacco for over three thousand fur pelts. The superiority of the cheapest, crudest metal ax over the finest stone ax attracted the Indians to trade. Firearms were traded for a stack of furs piled as high as a standing rifle. The Russians did not deal in liquor, as the Hudson Bay Company and John Jacob Astor had done.

For ten years, Derabin, as Russian administrator, carried on a lucrative fur trade marked by extreme cruelty to the natives. Indians still remember stories of how the Russians whipped men for any infraction. It culminated in the massacre of the entire garrison by northern Koyukuk Indians.

Two bands of Koyukons had long been at odds, plundering each other's camps. In 1846, the Nulato Koyukons had raided the northern camp, which years later would seek revenge.

In 1851, Lieutenant Barnard of the H.M.S. *Enterprise* arrived at Nulato seeking information about the fate of the famous explorer Sir John Franklin. According to scientist William H. Dall, Barnard remarked bluntly in the presence of Indians that he intended to send for the chief of the Koyukons, who was then celebrating a festival twenty-five miles from Nulato. That unfortunately worded remark was conveyed to the chief, who was not accustomed to being "sent for." When the Russians wanted to see him they "respectfully requested the honor of his presence." Ivan Bulegin, a Russian Indian, and a Nulato Indian were sent to see if they could bring the chief to Nulato but never returned.

Soon thereafter, a northern Koyukon war party, according to Dall, surrounded the underground Nulato homes of some one hundred unsuspecting men, women and children. They heaped their birch-bark canoes, paddles and snowshoes over the entrances to the houses and smoke holes, and set them aflame.

The unfortunate Nulato people, awakened by the noise and crackling of the flames, vainly tried to escape through the fire but were mercilessly shot down by the arrows; others suffocated in the smoke. A few women were taken by the victors, some men fled to the mountains and one or two children were able to save themselves in the woods. Some victims then tried with axes to cut their way out but were shot down by arrows. Since no guns were used and the screams of the women were stifled inside their underground houses, the massacre was accomplished without waking the Russians in the nearby post.

Next the northern Koyukons went to the trading post and repaid Derabin's brutality to the Indians by stabbing him to death as he cowered in his blankets. A Russian interpreter fell in the doorway, pierced by seven arrows. Lieutenant Barnard was stabbed repeatedly by the shaman and his brother until he fell back, mortally wounded.

Then the northern Koyukons attacked the Russians' homes. The Russians aimed their shots over the Indians' heads, hoping to avoid bloodshed. Back flew a shower of arrows.

One of the Russians the Indians had overlooked had lain in bed with fever. His wife, an Indian woman, brought him a loaded pistol and held him up while he fired at the shaman with trembling hands, wounding him. Another Russian shot an Indian, and at that point the war party retreated.

The last to die in the bloody massacre was a woman whom the wounded shaman happened upon by the riverbank. The woman was towing a sled with her child on it when the shaman threw the baby from the sled and ordered her to pull him back to camp. She refused and he knifed her to death.

She was the final victim of the Nulato massacre and of the old antipathy between the upper northern Koyukons and the Nulato Koyukons. Lieutenant Barnard died in agony before help could reach him, even though the Russians had tried to sew up his wounds.

The shaman survived and continued to be a frequent visitor at the post. According to Father Jules Jetté, a Jesuit who lived at Nulato forty-seven years later, the massacre of the people of Nulato by the Koyukon Indians was not due to the insult which the Koyukuk chief felt he had suffered by Lieutenant Barnard's remark, as Dall had reported; rather, it was an expression of the traditional rivalry.

Jetté, the Jesuit priest and ethnographer, observed that "these natives had no chiefs, nor recognized authority, until some five years ago." When the Russians first arrived, they needed one person to be responsible for trading and for maintaining law and order in the settlement; they were the ones who named the chief. Before that, Indians had prided themselves on being people without elected, appointed or hereditary leaders to whom obedience or submission was due. Jetté felt that Dall's story was an injustice to the Koyukons, an invention of the Russians to exonerate themselves before the British government, which took a dim view of the fact that one of its officers was killed while he was the Russians' guest.

The Russians rebuilt the stockade fort, with the graves of Barnard and Derabin behind it. The excavations where the Indian houses stood are still to be seen, and they formed the graves of those who perished in the massacre.

I could not find Lieutenant Barnard's marker at the graveyard. Set high up on the bluff was the miniature city of tin-roofed spirit houses, Russian white crosses, little burial houses and tall poles with balls marking graves. Like a silent army advancing, the ancestors' grave houses were slipping down the bluff, jolted by frost heaves.

The little houses, containing some treasure belonging to the dead, were placed over the graves. Sometimes a small table was set and food brought. Poldine Carlo of Nulato told of the woman who had her accordion buried with her. Every time there was a dance in the village, villagers borrowed her accordion for the night, replacing it the next day.

A fishwheel across the river made eerie sounds, the wheel creaking as it turned. The fishwheel, a wooden frame with scoops that rotated by the river current, caught and tossed fish into a side chute, where they were kept in the water. When the Indians saw the first fishwheel, invented by white men, they quickly adopted it. A single day's catch equaled a month's work by other methods, and it revolutionized the fishing economy, enabling Indians to feed larger dog teams. Fish became the staple food, as the use of firearms had resulted in the decrease of caribou.

Indians greeted the arrival of the first fish in the spring with prayers and incantations, for if the fish did not appear in sufficient numbers, hunger would follow. The first salmon that was caught was brought to the beach. The people gathered around it in joy and gratitude, dipping willow twigs into the water and sprinkling the fish, intoning, *"Kon Ne Midoya Tolitih,"* or "Come and stay with us." With the coming of the fishwheel the ceremony disappeared, as it had become impossible to know which fish was caught first.

After a warm summer's day, when the sun sets in a red sky, the glare of twilight reflected on the Yukon is called *Kat-Lo-Kona,* or "blood of the king salmon." It was said to last as long as the king salmon were running.

The women worked hard at fish camps, cutting fish all day long. The fish were cut into strips and hung in the smokehouse to dry. They also ripened fish heads for a change of diet. Cleaned salmon heads were placed over a layer of salmon eggs in a basket, then kept in the smokehouse for several weeks. The heads would turn green; the taste was similar to that of ripened cheese.

Olivia Esmailka's house was surrounded by a wooden walk. A spry, wrinkled lady of eighty-nine, she sat on her cot and plucked an enormous goose. Dangling from her earlobes were long gold nuggets and on her legs brown wool stockings. As she plucked the goose, it became smaller and smaller until it was one-third its size, a small pink-gray withered thing with limp legs and dangling head.

Riverboats were docked along the muddy beach. Wooden fish racks laden with dog salmon hung like orange laundry. Driftwood, empty oil barrels for trash burning, and staked huskies spotted the riverfront. Hillsides behind the village were dark, with tinges of gold. It had been raining and the river reflected the aspens; leaves hung by their stems as they twirled in the wind.

A woman in a heavy green parka and shirt, woolen stockings and red kerchief waved to her man, who took off in his motorboat, leaving a wake. Another woman was coming home with a basketful of cranberries.

Smoke poured out of a haphazard collection of small gray log cabins, caches, doghouses and outhouses. Buzz-saw sounds and distant barking punctured the air. The owners' names were written on wooden signs over the doorways: SIPIRY, CRISPIN ESMAILKA, DEMOSKI—Russian names.

Grandma lived in a tiny log house with a curtain partitioning one-quarter of the space for sleeping quarters. The matriarch had a full, kindly face and spoke English well.

All of her relatives seemed to be visiting—a jovial man who was slightly tipsy, two middle-aged women, a young mother, her three children, and a two-year-old baby boy, the family favorite—representing the four generations.

Grandma said that I was the first artist they had ever seen.

"I am proud to be the first artist," I answered. "Would you like me to do a painting of you?"

She agreed and I began. Evidently this was going to be the afternoon's entertainment. Everyone was interested and friendly as they gathered around to watch me. I was fascinated with the composition around Grandma, and oblivious of everyone, I began to paint, talking to them all the while about the children and village life.

She posed in her chair by the window near her half-barrel Yukon stove, her woodpile stacked near the wall, a huge teakettle on the stove. I liked the arrangement of practical things behind the stove on a shelf. There was not much in the way of foodstuff visible except the standard Hills Brothers coffee and pilot bread.

While I was painting, there were all kinds of interruptions in the small cabin. A youngster climbed over me to get his fishing pole. The black-haired baby ran all around me for about an hour, almost knocking over my paint box several times. A woman from Koyukuk came in to visit. Evidently news had spread that I was there, performing with colors and paints.

The women ribbed the jovial man, who announced that he wanted to take his boat out. "Moose hunting?" I asked.

"More like liquor hunting. Moose, huh!" snorted Grandma.

I painted a young girl next and thought about Athabaskan traditions regarding a young girl at puberty, which were the same, with some variations, up and down the Yukon. In the past the girl had to spend six months to a year in isolation behind the "blanket" or "moose hood." She could not look at the river or at any man, as it would bring bad luck in hunting. In some places she had to sit with her legs crossed under her, wearing a porcupine amulet to bring her luck. A restricted diet of dried food was enforced by an older woman or her grandmother.

Menstrual blood was thought to contain the essence of womanhood, and any contact would make a man unfit for hunting. A menstruating woman was not supposed to sleep with her husband or eat fresh meat or fish. The superstitions were due to fear of famine.

Most old women would rarely speak of the puberty ceremonies, but Vivian Peter remembered her youth.

"An old lady came into my tent with a cup of fish oil. I finally took it from her, closed my eyes, and in one gulp it was down . . . All summer, dried fish, dried meat was my diet. They were in a bag by my bed. I was told never to look at the Yukon River. It never entered my mind to go out and look at the river, either. I just stayed in the tent with my legs under me in a sitting position. We were not allowed to drink water in a cup. I had tied around my neck a piece of bone, the leg part of a crane [or swan]. I drank through that . . . Also tied to the same string was a beaver tooth. Before I eat I rub the tooth against my teeth. Now I don't have any teeth of my own.

"All during the summer, as much fish as there was, never once did I have a bite of fresh fish—just plain dried fish. No meat, just porcupine. I didn't eat berries until after two years were up. The reason for this [was that] the berries look so pretty for a while, but they don't last and then get wrinkled and fall off. So the saying 'You will not be pretty long if you eat berries. You will get old and wrinkled right away.'

"Another thing my aunt told me was 'Don't ever talk to boys or laugh with them. You will have a baby.' I was so afraid of that that I just wouldn't talk with boys."

In the upper Tanana, the girls lived by themselves about two miles away from the village for about five months. The moose-skin hood, decorated with porcupine-quill work or beadwork, was sometimes so heavy that it had to be tied to poles to keep it from falling, said one woman.

To a girl it was the most important rite of passage in her life, because after her ritual period she would be ready for marriage. When the initiation was over, she was given a new set of clothes. She was supposed to have a face like snow, hair like a raven's wing, her figure slim and her sewing basket full. Her parents now could select a husband for her, a man who would work hard for several years, hunting and living with them in their house. If the shaman wanted her, he had first choice because of his powers.

It seemed to me that the girl would be glad to leave her isolation after eating dried food for a year. The regimen did produce strong, hard-working, uncomplaining, self-sacrificing women who had to obey their men and the taboos. If a girl did not follow the law, punishment was severe—ridicule or sometimes death.

Women in those days, according to Father William Loyens, a Jesuit social anthropologist who lived in Nulato for two years, could not eat the lips of rabbits "lest they get twitching lips." Yet the female porcupine, who was considered wise, with a highly developed sense of smell and keen eyes, was permissible as food but only dried, not fresh. During beaver trapping, the wife had to be busy or the man would not trap any beaver. Woman could not eat the pelvic region or thighs of a beaver lest they have difficult childbirth. Beaver bones had to be thrown into the river with the words "Be made again in the water."

Young women in later days were segregated by a blanket around their bed in a corner of the cabin. The hood was dispensed with and the women began to wear scarves on their heads during the menses. Today the young girls under the influence of the church and school do not have to go through the old rituals.

What did I understand, a white woman used to the life of modern comfort? I tried to put myself in her place, a girl used to running in the forests, attuned to the seasons and living with fear of the unknown, the fear of starvation, needing to contribute to the cycle of life in order to be a member of the group. The basic need was to attract a man to hunt and to perpetuate the small group by giving birth. Had I been such a woman, with a shaman or old woman instructing me, sacrificing one year sitting in a shelter, eating dried food and drinking water through a swan's leg bone, becoming strong, beautiful of spirit, having enough to eat all my life, guaranteed a good husband who could supply me with all my needs, would I have done the same?

The children surrounded me. "Do me, do me," they clamored, asking me to paint them. Some of them, even the seven-year-olds, chewed Copenhagen snuff. They traveled in a pack, plaguing the storekeeper's little dog unmercifully. An eight-year-old carried a sharp hunting knife without a sheath in his pocket.

The postmistress, Josephine Mountain, who had broad cheek-bones, offered to pose. The little critics, when they saw my sketch, screamed, "She looks Eskimo." When I drew another woman the chorus shouted approval: "Indian, Indian." One woman introduced me to her "four bad little Indians."

Many of the children wore Indian headbands. One sturdy boy with a blue kerchief tied around his forehead was the leader of the group.

In the past, boys did not have elaborate puberty rites. From the time the boy was turned over to his uncle at six, he was inured to every hardship of cold to develop his powers of endurance. He learned the best ways of hunting, trapping, fishing, making tools and snowshoes, and building shelter. He snowshoed all day, following the hunters. His first kill was marked by a feast. Some boys searched for medicine or guardian spirits by fasting and wandering alone in in the woods. They would establish friendly relations with some animal which they were not allowed to kill, even when they were hungry. It was thought, in future times of need or danger, the animal might then offer his aid.

I asked Ken Silas, the boy with the blue kerchief, to come aboard and pose for me, as the children were so noisy I could not concentrate.

We climbed aboard the gangplank, and I showed him around the boat and introduced him to Dave Walker. Ken walked proudly, striding with his hands in his jeans pockets. It was no small feat to be selected to come aboard the biggest boat he had ever seen. Adriana fed him milk and a peanut-butter sandwich, which he saved in a napkin, and Agnes gave him cookies and oranges in a sack.

It turned out to be the best portrait I had painted on the trip. His fine-boned face held a serious expression, intelligent and vulnerable, emphasized by a strong chin. He wore a blue jacket and his hair was held back by a blue bandanna. He was a cooperative model.

Before I gave him some money, I asked what he would do with it. "Buy Coke," he said. I tried to persuade him to buy food instead. There were ten people in his family; his father was dead and his mother worked hard.

The children were waiting for their leader, clambering over him to find out what had happened. I was pleased to hear the children speaking in Koyukon when Ken took them into the store. They all came out drinking Cokes.

I walked down to the Catholic church, which the villagers had built, including the altar and benches. They had bought the copper tabernacle, the piano and the plaster statues. Over the altar was an old sign reading, FATHER SEGHERS WAS MURDERED HERE.

Father McDonough, the resident priest, his face ashen, was suffering from a cold. Attendance at church had dropped off considerably; mainly the old people were faithful.

Father William Loyens, the social anthropologist, once calculated the salaries from all sources in Nulato and came to the conclusion that the average family of six lived on less than the average American individual! (In 1965 the average United States citizen's income was $2,727.) Ninety percent of the men of Nulato were unemployed, but next year there would be employment on the new high school. A carpenter's apprentice would receive $5.50 per hour.

Without jobs, families had to depend on welfare. In spite of the Bureau of Indian Affairs' efforts to relocate people in the States, Indians preferred to stay in their villages. Life in the village, despite the poverty, seemed to be preferable to an unhappy life among white strangers in big cities.

Father McDonough and I also spoke of Father Jetté, who served at Nulato from 1898 to 1908. A man of wide general culture, master of four languages and a mathematician, Jetté wrote a dictionary containing 2,344 pages of the Koyukon language and spoke so fluently and vigorously that Indians traveled many miles just to hear him speak.

Jetté wrote to his superior: "The people are of a kind, genial and very sensitive disposition. The least token of friendship goes to their hearts as well. Unfortunately, gambling and drinking, two gifts of our civilization, have speedily taken root among these people."

"My shabby clothes," wrote the most distinguished scholar in Alaska, "and boyish manners were the cause of being dubbed 'a bum priest.' "

If Father Tosi, who built the first mission at Nulato, could be resurrected, he would note with satisfaction the disappearance of the shaman. The shaman was said to have been able to foretell the future, cure illness, perform amazing feats and control the people through fear and power.

Zagoskin, a Russian explorer, had come upon a camping party and its sled dogs one night. The Indians were sleeping, covered with caribou skins, under the shelter of spruce branches, with their sleds, snowshoes, fish traps and other gear strewn about. They awoke and performed a welcome ceremony for him.

"They faced east, pulled falcon feathers from their hair, held them in both hands and sang, leaning forward with the whole body and stamping with the right foot. An older man with rumpled hair strewn with eagle down began to stagger about. He jerked and muttered words, then began to bark and yelp, 'to howl like a wolf,' to caw like a crow, like a magpie. Foam churned out of his mouth . . . I felt depressed. What is this? I wondered," wrote Zagoskin. "Simply an ordinary dance or the indication of a bond between man and the world of the unseen?"

Father Loyens wrote that the people had believed in the spirits of the cold and wind and in the spirits of human souls considered to be immortal, waiting for reincarnation. There were evil spirits such as goblins, people of rocks and air, water and fire spirits. There was also a *"yega"* spirit that threatened calamity on anyone who disobeyed it. Spirits governed the run of salmon, the bears and other animals of the north who struggled for existence.

There was a need for one who had power over evil spirits, who, by incantations and charms of magic, could control the powers who worked against the people. Thus the shamans, or medicine men, derived power, making ceremonies to control destiny, acting as mediators between the people and the supernatural world. The shaman called for good weather, good fish runs, good hunting, success in warfare and relief in time of famine or trouble. Taboos, magic of all varieties, ritual songs, myths and rigid protocols protected the people through life crises from birth to death. All gave what most religions give—a certain security through appeal to the powers beyond that are greater than human powers.

Amulets such as hawk's eyes threaded with sinew were worn as protection on parkas to help prevent snowblindness. The largest feather of the raven was tied to the child's hair, enabling him to run fast, and a porcupine heart was eaten to gain courage.

Shamans cured people by blowing and sucking, going into trances, using drums and masks, and conversing with the spirit world. Some practitioners had a lot of paraphernalia, including elaborate caribou-skin parkas which had claws and beaks that rattled when the wearer danced. Shamans had soul catchers, tubes of carved bone that they sucked, spirit headbands and drums. The shaman would sing his spirit songs until he shook, his eyes rolled and, according to some informants, he floated above the ground. With the help of spirits, the shaman extracted illness in the form of a piece of bone. Sometimes the problem was a patient's soul that had been stolen or harmed by an offended animal or hostile shaman. In some cases the patient could not be helped and his payment was returned.

Bob Simpson, Nulato schoolteacher, came aboard, looking for the ceramic tile he had ordered. It was not on the boat and this was the barge's last trip of the year. In the bush tradition, he said that if I wished to stay in Nulato, I could stay with him and his wife. He invited me to visit, and tired as I was, I tromped through the village mud, following him to the end of the village, where he had his trailer home.

Inside the trailer were a couch, rugs, modern kitchen complete with plumbing, records and sculpture; the walls were decorated with the skins of two lynx and a wolverine. What impressed me was a copy of the Sunday New York *Times* lying there, albeit a month late in transit. His wife, Elizabeth, a young black woman, was also a school-teacher. We talked about books and life in Nulato. When I went home that night, Elizabeth led the way with a flashlight, as it was dark, huskies were loose and the path was invisible.

I scampered down muddy banks, past the forklift and the dragline, onto the wet, slippery, one-foot-narrow gangplank, then carefully walked across the puddles and strung cable on the barge, trying to avoid falling into the dark river. And so to bed with back issues of the New York *Times Book Review* that Elizabeth had kindly given me.

The next day the sky was absolutely white, as always before snow-fall. It was depressing, a penetrating-to-the-bone feeling. Everyone aboard felt low in spirits. I forced myself to go up on deck and paint the graveyard with its white crosses and the fish racks below. Dogs staked at the banks were being fed, making their yelping sounds and straining against their ropes.

Later, as darkness fell, the church steeple was outlined by a pink-violet sunset, a soft rosy color. I heard the children calling "Clara, Clara" from the banks as they waved to me and the boat began to move, leaving behind the dark silhouette of Nulato against the dimming light.

Months later, I met Mrs. Mountain in Fairbanks, and she told me about Ken Silas. "All of Therese Silas' nine kids could swim and do all kinds of athletics," she began. "The younger brother was swimming in the Yukon with Ken and his nephew. They swam to a little island, but the brother panicked. Ken tried to save him, but he was dragged under by the current. Ken, his brother and nephew all drowned. They found their pile of clothes by the shore. Other kids below town heard them hollering, but it was too late, they were too far."

Kenneth Silas, with all his leadership qualities, was only thirteen.

CHAPTER 11

Kaltag

When I was a kid they trained us to jump
out of bed barefooted and chased us out to
make water on the snow, forty below zero.
Run before breakfast. Don't lay down after
you eat, don't drink water with your meals.
Don't eat before the race, no meat. That's
the way I was trained. I ran ahead of dog
teams forty-six miles to Ruby, another time
thirty miles to Nulato.

    Too much schooling is no good. You get
too smart for nothing and lazy. You live
longer if you use your muscles like me. Well,
I guess I am through working for the rest of
my life. A man that's sixty-six years old
should have it made. Although I haven't,
I'm going to take it easy and live off the
land—that is, if the game wardens leave me
alone . . . I'm not buying any more license
to trap my own ground.

FRED STICKMAN, SR.,
letter to the editor,
Fairbanks News-Miner

THE next boat stop, the village of Kaltag, stretched out along the riverbank. The road shone with last night's rain, and gray-blue smoke drifted, dispersing the scent of burning wood. Snow fell on the mountaintops; the foothills were a blueberry color.

Bells rang out from a wooden building resembling a stockade with a bullet-shaped steeple topped with a cross.

Children raced along the shore, for they knew that candy was coming to the store. Stacks of oil barrels were piled high along the beach near fish racks and two old skiffs. Men sauntered down the hill, hands in their pockets, with two terriers, huskies and a small chihuahua following. No cats.

In winter the villagers dumped refuse on the river ice. During the spring breakup, the Yukon, like the proverbial garbage collector, swept it all away. Sometimes the trash remained on the beach, leaving rusting cans once full of Hawaiian Punch and Pepsi. This time of year, however, the beach was clean.

It was the river life of the people that I liked, especially the children, who seemed to belong to no one and everyone. The children followed me as if I were the Pied Piper. They had the freedom to run about and there was little traffic to worry about, yet I wondered how many got lost in the woods or fell off the steep bank into the river.

The children hollered when I passed around bubble gum, their brown hands stretched open: "I ain't got nawthin'." A truck loaded down with Coke cans, a symbol of modern civilization, sank into the mud in front of the store and came to a trembling, snorting halt. The storekeeper told me the shipment would not last long. Coke is status. In Minto ten cases lasted three days. In Kaltag the store had seventeen thousand dollars credit on the books.

A woman died last week, beaten to death by her husband in a drunken furor. "They'll never stop drinking," a young woman stated flatly. "Too damn many get suicidal and too damn many freeze to death. Get in accidents. Drink too much. They drink up their welfare money. My brother froze to death. This young generation is lost between white and Indian." Alcohol is dis-ease, the symptoms of which affect Yukon River life. One of the symptoms is the suffering of the children.

Alex Solomon, president of the Kaltag village council, has worked as a carpenter and commercial fisherman and, in the winter, trapped marten and mink. With nine children to feed he used every resource the land provided. "We have a run of eels under the ice," he said, drinking a Coke. "We find out when they are coming upriver, then we catch them in dip nets. When I put a stick in the river, they wrap themselves around it. When we feed eels to the dogs they get fat on it; it's just like eating bacon. The eels get thinner and thinner as they go upriver. When the channel is narrow and there are good feeding grounds, the eels get so thick that the river rises and I can get them with just a stick."

Eels taste similar to sardines. They are usually roasted or pan-fried on the Yukon, but in Europe jellied or smoked eels are a delicacy.

Another Athabaskan delicacy is "mouse nuts," the wild potato roots found cached in the nests of mice. The women cook the white root with bear grease. They use wild celery, wild rhubarb and caribou moss for spring greens. Sap from the birches is a sweet change of diet.

"We like to live off the land and go hunting," Alex said. "More people are coming up here. I don't like it much. This whole place used to be ours. We traveled with the fish. In early September we'd split fish, green fish, unsmoked. We'd clean it and hang it.

"They'll be putting up gas stations in Kaltag next! Our life is changing too fast."

A young boy described his first impression of a trip to Seattle: "Honking, blurry cars, miles and miles of pavement. Blurry people in the same style of clothing. The same J. C. Penney or Woolworth's store on Main Street. Everything manufactured yesterday out of plastic."

He commented on our prized modern roads: "They're going to have a terrible time getting all that gray hard stuff off the grass." He had never seen in his world any "gray hard stuff" covering the earth. To him it was some blight or disease.

"The teachers know a lot from books," he said. "But my uncle says Indians been here thousands of years, long before planes, and if white people had to live without gadgets, they wouldn't know what to do. They'd die."

Their teachers had talked about the oil pipeline and he was afraid of an oil spill. I agreed with him. "If a pipe breaks," he said, "and the oil spills, our animals would die, fish would be poisoned and ducks would get crippled from oil on their feathers. I saw it in a magazine."

Beverly Madros, at ten, had never been more than a hundred miles out of her village. Beverly, who had ten brothers and sisters, learned about the outside world at school or from strangers like me. She sat for her portrait gracefully, her hair an electric blue-black inky color, heavy with shimmering lights. Her skin had orange-gold tints from the rich blood coursing through her. The portrait did not do her justice and I felt sorry that the great photographer Edward S. Curtis could not have been there.

Captain Art took me to see the storekeeper's dog sled hanging in the shed from the ceiling. The storekeeper would not sell it, saying he had to ask his wife, who was in Nulato.

At Kaltag no one had cut wood for the winter, although snowfall was a week away. "At two in the morning, I'd hear dogs howl," said Captain Art. Indians would hitch up the dog team and away they would speed on their sleds to come back with some wood. Soon smoke would be coming out of their chimneys. "After all," the captain mused, "why cut wood for tomorrow? I may not be alive then."

Most white men think differently about this woodcutting business and feel a need for security. Does this prove that the Indians feel secure in their own land and the white men insecure? Only two generations ago Indians were nomads stopping to camp. "If you are migrating, why save up a woodpile? You can't take it with you," I responded.

Captain Art was a mine of information about everything. I liked to watch him roam the village, walking loosely, talking to everyone and enjoying every minute. He informed me that first ice crystals formed on the Yukon, then "pancakes," his term for flat cakes of ice, and then they joined together. It was a time for rejoicing when the rivers become solidly frozen, because then the people could travel easily to hunt and the plague of mosquitoes and gnats would be over until next year.

We talked about the Bergland girls. "Those two sisters worked harder than men! They were tough as nails. They trapped out of Fort Yukon, living out on their trap lines all winter."

I had met the girls once in Fairbanks, heavy-shouldered white women doing men's work. The girls would have died as children, for their father was sick and they were destitute. The mother took them out in a boat to drown them. An old man saved them and brought them out on his trap line, where they learned to trap and fend for themselves in the wilderness. They could drive a dog team and trap all winter in the most severe weather, cut up a moose and pack it home, carrying the haunches on their backs. Thirty miles of snowshoeing was nothing to them. Captain Art recalled, "When Hazel hitched up the dogs, the air turned blue. No mule-skinner had it over her."

Kaltag was known for its "washtub dance." People would sing as they carried a large canvas, going from house to house to collect dried fish, canned goods, homemade bread and bundles of frozen fish. At the dance, their drum was a plastic-covered washtub.

I had read anthropologist Cornelius Osgood's description of a "hot dance" held years ago in the Anvik area. The men sang a hot-dance song in the woods as they prepared a spruce tree by stripping it and decorating it with feathers and red stripes. This pole was lowered from the roof into the smoke hole of the *kashim*, the ceremonial bathhouse. The men, with wolf skins on their heads, would grab the pole and dance with bent knees in a circle.

At midnight the lamps were covered with wooden bowls, and each man headed for the woman he liked, not his own wife, wrote Osgood. In the darkness that followed there was much laughing and squealing. After a warning the lamps were uncovered and the people sang and danced again.

At dawn the men climbed the pole, pulled it out through the smoke hole and threw it behind the *kashim*, which was the signal for everyone to go home.

They still do the washtub dance, but I wondered if they ever did the hot dance anymore. In the house journal of the Jesuits of December 25, 1912, I read: "We were told that the Indians were preparing a big potlatch in honor of the dead and were going to dress a girl around whom, while stripped, they were to dance. The Indians were therefore told that we would have no Christmas celebration unless they promised to give up that horrible practice. They did not want to promise, so we had no midnight Mass."

The Jesuits also found the Feast of the Dead and the stick dance incompatible with Christianity. The ritual, after all, helped the deceased on his way to an eternity where no judgments of good and evil were made. Nowadays the priest attends the stick dance and conducts the funeral.

Missouri Stanley, known as an outstanding singer at the stick dances, had just returned from his fish nets one and a half miles upriver. Missouri, named by a white schoolteacher exasperated with Koyukon phonetics, resembled Popeye, with pipe in mouth and grizzled beard. Bent, crippled, over his meager woodpile, he could not straighten up anymore. His arm trembled in pain as he slowly chopped each piece, his head held to one side.

His wife, Anastasia, her careworn face hidden in her kerchief, went out to cut a washtub load of fish they had caught, mostly chinooks and whitefish. Her thin, hunched shoulders were covered by a black threadbare coat several sizes too large. Her shrunken body held a toughness bred in her bones from hard work. She had once been the village beauty.

I helped her carry the washtub of fish to a rickety table near a broken-down shed used for smoking fish. I offered her an orange and then sat down on a pile of old lumber. Anastasia, her arms bloody to the elbow, cut fish with her freshly whetted, curved woman's knife. I admired her performance, knowing how clumsy I was with a knife. Orange salmon swung by their tails from her pole drying rack. A huge rat ran out from under the woodpile I was sitting on and I leaped into the air.

The old couple invited me into their little home, which contained a double bed with a bare mattress, a table, a stove and two broken-down chairs—that was all, no other amenities. The absence of possessions, after working all their lives, showed me the hand-to-mouth struggle of day-to-day existence on the Yukon. Then I realized I saw their cabin from a white viewpoint and that my judging their absence of possessions reflected my materialistic view. These people lived by other values, from a time when their ancestors carried all they owned on their backs.

A little girl whose mother had died last week was going to live with her sister in Fairbanks. I wondered if it was her mother who had been beaten to death. The child followed me in my wanderings, holding my hand as we went into the old church. The inner room was in darkness. Moose legs were stacked on the storm porch. Evidently the church was occupied, since a boy was at home; he told us the family had gone to a funeral in Nulato.

If a woman was left a widow in the early days, she could marry again, depending on the tribe. If they pointed at her and said she could not marry again, that was the law. I wondered how they arrived at that decision. What constituted a bad wife? Barren? Unfaithful? Poor skin sewer?

If a woman was found with another man, the offended husband had the right to throw her out or beat or stab her, but there was no censure if the offender was the man. There was a double standard.

Years ago widowed women were scorned, left to wander the village ragged and poor, often beaten and starved. In some places the poor woman had to carry around the bones of her husband in a bag.

On the Yukon, Athabaskan women used to cut gashes in their thighs and cut their hair after their husbands died. The Sekani Indians of Canada, also Athabaskan, cut off their fingers in grief, sometimes in cases of disappointed love. I read about one woman who had all but two fingers gone, attesting to her suffering.

I thought of the huge rat I saw that day and wondered if it was a lemming. Anastasia said it was not a year for lemmings, as they came every seven years.

One of the strangest spectacles seen in Kaltag was the lemmings' migration over the river ice. The small bewitched rodents followed their instincts to their death. In the spring a seemingly emotional mob hysteria swept over them as they left first in small bands, then in larger groups. They swept down gullies, across ponds and over hills to the frozen river. Then their migration worked itself up to a frenzy as they crossed the rivers in the thousands, paddling furiously to reach the opposite banks. Hordes of lemmings covered the Yukon River's rotten ice, slush dragging their feet.

For months during their trek they continued, bearing young, eating, never stopping until exhaustion dulled their drive. As they slept, predators killed many of them. The next year there would appear to be no lemmings, and their enemies would grow lean and starve.

To reach Kaltag they crossed miniature thickets of dwarf willows, blueberry bushes, gullies and rivers. In Kaltag, on their seven-year cycle, the Indians shot them, and the dogs attacked and ate them.

When they reached the ice floes of the Bering Sea about ninety miles west of Kaltag, their final destination with death, they kept swimming until their strength was gone and they drowned.

It was a balmy night; sunset illuminated the poplars across the river. I could hear wild geese gabble, thick and choppy on the wind, their call raucous. A bonfire flared up on the beach, and when I went to investigate it, I discovered that a six-year-old had poured gasoline from a motorboat onto a pile of driftwood. The child was unharmed by the flames. I put out the fire with water and bawled him out.

I saw the priest, who had recently arrived in Kaltag, taking a walk on the beach. Did the children want to emulate him, I wondered, when he swallowed the wafer and drank the wine in front of the village?

It was difficult to part with the children. I had to shake hands with everyone before I could leave and walk to the boat. The children wanted me to repeat their names so I would remember each one of them. Later I sent Beverly Madros, the ten-year-old who posed for me, a pendant for posing and she wrote me a touching letter. Strangers came and went, touching their lives so briefly.

Would Beverly spend her life within the village confines, raising ten children like her mother, or would she go "outside" to school and never return? At school she would be taught to take a shower every day, then would return to a village without running water. However, the village teachers lived in homes with plumbing and running water. There were no Indian schoolteachers for her to emulate, nor were there many jobs for young women in the village.

The children stood on the banks watching me. How I wished I could give them a more tangible affirmation of their strengths. We watched each other, waving until the darkness and water separated us from sight.

CHAPTER 12

Grayling

My older sister, they say it's good up that way.
Go there,
Take all your relatives with you.
Take them all with you to that good place.
My older sister, they say it's good up that way,
Go there.

SHOOT'OO YAHAN'S SONG
upon the death of her sister

THE river left its mark against the shore, strewing logs, ripping them apart, dashing them on the narrow beach. The earth was a reddish clay with a coal-like substance near the white rock outcroppings. Yellow lacy leaves made patterns against the brown hills.

The decks were drying from rain as we headed toward a narrow channel, passing a golden island called Morgan. I pored over the ship's map with Captain Art. The huge green map had blue tree marks for hills and riverways. "At a place called Stink Creek near here, our boat,

The Rampart, crashed into the shore and had to be pulled out," said Captain Art.

The map marked places called Steamboat Slough, Eagle Slide, Honeymoon Slough, Bullfrog Island, Old Woman River, Papa Willie Creek, Devil's Elbow, Yokontoh Slough, Shovel Creek, Holikachuk, Fat John Slough and Dogfish Village. There are fifty-seven Bear Creeks in Alaska!

Where the Yukon empties out into the Bering Sea there is a place called Tin Can Point. This countryside must have had a going over by prospectors carrying backpacks full of canned food. Summers must have seen boats and rafts up and down the Yukon. Ruby and Koyukuk had many gold seekers who sank holes into the countryside.

Flocks of geese had been feeding on the sand bars but rose when we turned into the bend of an island. A winter dog-team trail paralleled the river, and tall bluffs and bleached-white driftwood lined the banks.

I read peacefully on my cot in the midst of a two-mile-wide churning river mad with whitecaps and wind. The boat jerked back and forth while the river raged like an ocean.

In the afternoon I painted in my small room. The light from the bulb was poor, but the wild river outside gave me a fierce energy, and I strengthened all the forms and colors. It was a good day's work.

I do not feel I could paint with such inspired feeling and power outside of Alaska. This land and its people give to me. I can feel its roots surging out of the earth through its people. It is a privilege to be among them, feeling so harmoniously alive.

Dark trees appeared close to the window and a gray fog showed a solitary gull. I felt a sense of overpowering wilderness, as if no one had stepped on this land before. We were getting closer to the sea, farther away from home. In my imagination I could dimly make out in the heavy fog Indians paddling birch-bark canoes in unison.

This low countryside would soon be shrouded in snow and ice. Fog obscured the farthest mountains, and the close hills were the color of sienna and faded browns. Bears and moose roamed these hillsides, and smaller animals inhabited the earth holes and caverns.

This was the forest primeval: birches with white trunks, tundra berries and leaf mold. Strange twisted tree forms shed their bright covering leaves. The morning seemed pristine and clean, the banks wet from rain.

The channels opened and disappeared from view as the boat moved, the water opening as if to secret hidden places mysteriously beckoning. Land closed behind me and left no way out, as thick foliage concealed the entrance. Only Indians knew the secret places.

Indians possessed the strange sense of place by the way their toes gripped the earth when they stood or walked. I noticed this while watching Anastasia wield her knife, her legs firmly planted, severing salmon heads on her crude table. Indians boiled and savored the fish heads that white people discarded as waste. Indian children fought over moose bones, cracking them to suck out the marrow. Indian houses smelled of earth, fish, meat and wood fire.

Indian children had long, thick, black, greasy hair, and it shone blue in the firelight. The children had strong, full chins, their jaws powerful from chewing moose meat. Their teeth were white and strong; their voices had a hard, guttural sound. They spoke loudly in the villages, not shyly as I have heard them speak among white people in schools. The young Indians sat in their boats at ease, steering the motors as if they were an extension of them, going downstream wearing raggy jackets, their hair waving in the cold wind, then returning with meat in the boat.

Two boys in Kaltag carried a huge porcupine by the legs.

"What will you do with it?" I asked.

"Cook it. Make soup." Rabbit, muskrat, beaver, lynx, all went into the cook pot.

Lemon-colored slices streaked the lower sky and the hillsides. The river dashed against the shore, strewing more logs, and our clumsy barge moved ahead in the night, throwing a large wake.

The next morning the sun rose over the hills, dispeling the fog. I felt rested. The boat had become a shelter; the throb no longer seemed like noise, but had a musical rhythm. So sailors must feel.

Captain Art said that the river swells had been about three feet high yesterday. Today it was calm, and the fishwheels along the shore rotated lazily in the wind. The sun poured its silver light on stones, lichens and the wings of ravens.

We were approaching Grayling. "Indian Power" was painted on an overturned canoe lying on the beach. A few dwellings stood against the haze of gold birch with tall hills beyond. The running-river sounds mingled with the steady, slow strokes of an ax biting into a live tree trunk, and I smelled rotting leaves and earth.

Freshly painted green, yellow and red houses were set in a rural landscape resembling New England. These Indians, a very small group, had moved from Holikachuk with the aid of the government. The houses were on one-half acre of land, planned with tall trees and graveled roads. Grayling had raspberry plants and gardens of potatoes and turnips. Gnats bit my ankles.

I strolled along in my Cowichan sweater, with my sketch pad under my arm, until I came upon a man dressed in black, like a Spanish grandee. His black hat, worn with a flair, shadowed his swarthy, weather-beaten face.

The tall Spanish-looking gentleman with a mustache turned out to be John Deacon, whom Captain Art called "Mr. Grayling." Adriana had talked about John the whole trip, saying, "Wait until you meet John Deacon. He bridges the gap between two cultures and stands tall in both."

John Deacon had worked in mining camps for years, then ran his own lumber business and sawmill. I admired his large two-story log house, which he had built rather than accept government housing at low cost. At eighty-five he had a proud, straight back and dignified manner.

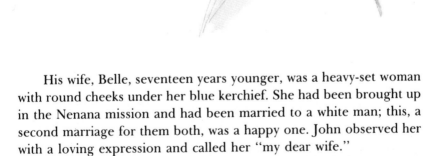

His wife, Belle, seventeen years younger, was a heavy-set woman with round cheeks under her blue kerchief. She had been brought up in the Nenana mission and had been married to a white man; this, a second marriage for them both, was a happy one. John observed her with a loving expression and called her "my dear wife."

They fished for salmon, hunted for moose and had a huge vegetable garden which fed them all year. Belle, known as the finest basket maker on the Yukon, showed me her prize-winning willow-root and birch-bark baskets. The birch was flawless and the willow, dyed in old reds and blues, made elaborate symmetrical designs along the edge.

She and John had selected the grasses by the riverbanks, "so strong it never breaks."

"I used to own and operate a sawmill. I used to worry about money," John said, "but I worry no more. I don't have a worry in the world." Looking at me with his penetrating black eyes, he said, "I had no education," meaning he had no formal schooling.

I looked him in the eye and called his bluff: "You know how to live. That's real education."

Evidently I passed the test, because he asked me if I would like to have a cup of coffee. We drank it in the kitchen and ate Belle's home-made cake while talking about village life and the poor potato crop.

We talked easily, with long silences, watching the birch leaves flutter in the wind, smelling the tang of autumn in the air. John summed up his life simply: "I'm ready to go anytime." There was no striving to be, just being.

In their cache hung the finest king salmon, smoked over a cotton-wood fire. Captain Peterson and I bought a bundle to take home and savor.

Henry Deacon, their nephew, came over to the mess house to join the captain for a cup of coffee. He said the men at Grayling had no work all summer; they lived on food stamps and welfare, buying meat in the store. "I wish sometime I wasn't working," he said, half-joking. "I could get food stamps too."

The general consensus here was that the land-claims money would go to some in the form of fat wages. "The money will go into pockets of a few people," said an Indian. "When the money is gone we'll be taxed for our land, and soon we'll lose our land, too, and wind up worse than before, with the old people getting nothing."

Captain Peterson had his own ideas: "The land-claims money should be used to educate Indian children. They need lawyers. The Tyonek Indians hired lawyers to invest their money, and they lost it through bad investments."

The schoolteachers said it was the best village they had ever been in—people had pride in their village and the children seemed cleaner and better dressed. At Grayling there was running water, indoor plumbing and a fine new school, plus a scenic view of the river. By the white man's standards it was an ideal village.

At New Year's the Indians danced, wearing masks similar to those of Point Hope, an Eskimo village I had visited. The fur parkas were also similar and the women used the same cutting tool. The Indians adapted many things from the Eskimos to the north.

Peter, the Episcopalian layman, a young man with a black beard, walked by, carrying three grouse hens and a gun slung over his back. The Episcopal log church was a comfortable two-story log house with the largest woodpile I had seen on the Yukon.

The Grayling of today seemed to be a peaceful village of plenty, but I heard tales of starvation and the horrors of the flu and the measle epidemics.

Dr. James White, medical officer on the steamer *Nunivak*, reported an epidemic and how it was treated at Grayling in 1901: "One woman had her neck and shoulders covered with scars," he wrote. "The skin is pricked rather deep with a knife or sharp stone and the wound kept open by frequent irritations until patient is well. When bleeding is resorted to, a vein is opened with a similar instrument."

It was either feast or famine along the Yukon. "My people know about starving," said David Paul, a lay minister. "I was raised in a country where we got no store. No trader. We hunt. White man came to the country, made life easier than it used to be. We had a good time before white man came here, but the dogs starved and we ourselves barely survived. Gone without eating for days." If no big game was available, Indians had to live on rabbits; if there were no rabbits, they lived on roots. "Some year come and no animals, no fish, no berries, just roots," Paul said. "Sometime in the old days he eat man he so hungry. Even his own people he eat sometime."

Cannibalism occasionally occurred, as it did among the Eskimos and white people during periods of starvation. At such times Indians survived by "making broth from boiled animal dung and by eating the inner bark of willows," David Paul said. "In the old days life was so hard that when the old people talked of it [cannibalism] they would burst into tears."

The horror of the epidemic is now mostly forgotten, lingering only in the memory of the old, like Olivia Esmailka, who told a story about an old woman named Meauska-layn, who lived with them. Every time Olivia gave her food to eat, she would protest, "You give me too much."

Meauska-layn was an orphan. "Always I got the backbone of fish. As winter had gone and spring was near I started getting less than before. I got weaker and weaker. The children would eat and eat. When spring came and water was running along the creeks, I got so weak that I could hardly walk. I had only water to drink. My face swelled and I couldn't get up. The children of these people were out playing all the time, having so much fun. I'd just sleep most of the time.

"I crawled into a birch-bark boat and got to the bow and lay on my old clothes. Next thing I knew I saw willows and trees on both sides and we were going down a slough. I heard someone real mad . . . A woman was standing there saying, 'What's wrong with you? Are you sick?' I just put my head down, didn't even move. She came, put her arms around and pulled me.

"Later on I found out she was a medicine woman. She brought my poor clothes up and put them where I could lay on them. All the time she was mad. Afterward, she brought me a little birch-bark bowl. In it was boiled fish. It was like soup. Also in it was a spoon. When did I ever see food like this? She put a spoonful in my mouth, just held it. The old medicine woman blew in the fish soup, also on my head and ears. She gave me about three spoons of the fish soup.

"I just went right to sleep. As she was leaving she said, 'I will leave this here and whenever you wake up take a spoonful at a time. Even though you are hungry, just eat a little at a time.' There was even some fish oil over the soup. As I woke up I'd take one or two spoons. Soon I noticed I was getting a little bit stronger."

Olivia said that when Meauska-layn told her story, she cried, saying, "Grandchild, it's for this reason even in the summertime, when there is so much fish, I don't ever want to step over fish guts. It's on account of the medicine woman that I am alive."

It was only a generation ago that people starved. At Grayling now children get school lunches and shots in school against epidemics; welfare checks see to it that no one starves to death anymore.

CHAPTER 13

Anvik

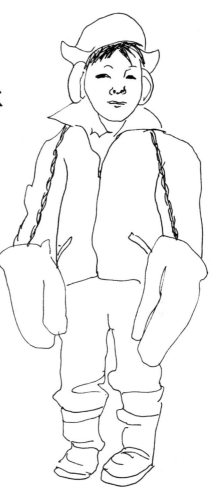

We heard stories about the bird no one kills,
the crow, who can change himself into
anything and who made the Yukon River by
drawing a furrow with his feet and the hills
and mountains by carrying earth . . .

When the caribou and deer began to
decrease at Anvik, the people also became
greatly alarmed. They were afraid it was
because of something they had done, and
they consulted the shaman. When he came
out of his trance he told them to paint seven
deer on the board over the ridgepole of the
grave building of a certain shaman who had
been a great hunter of caribou. Each deer
was to represent a year's kill. (Once, long
ago, to preclude hulang, the shaman
ordered a man to be thrown off the side of a
certain mountain.)

At every death the shaman has to give
the death stroke; that is, when it is time to
send the spirit of the deceased away—on the
fourth day for an ordinary person, some days
later for a person of distinction—the shaman
has to strike the corpse on the chest. He
sends him on his journey under the river to
the village of the spirits.

Cries-for-Salmon (Anvik boy),
collected by
DR. ELLIE CLEW PARSONS, 1920

THE village of Anvik, off a slough, is an old village with an artistic culture rich in myths, dances, songs and decorative arts. Anthropologists called the culture "Ingalik," an Eskimo word meaning lousy. The Indians, however, did not acknowledge the term; they said the Eskimos who lived on their borders called them Ingaliks. Although they warred with each other, they did exchange many customs.

A few houses are seen along the riverbanks, small grayed log cabins that had been through many floods. The modern schoolhouse was set back from the banks, and the young schoolteacher walked by with a load of dried salmon—for dogfood—on her back. The schoolchildren were let out early on account of the boat's arrival.

People lived in log cabins covered with weeds and wildflowers, even an occasional tree growing out from the sod roofs. A huge two-story log building with many windows, called the Mission, was used as a boarding school for Indian children. The First Episcopal Church in Alaska was established here; now it houses a caretaker and her son, who heated only her little room and blocked off the rest of the house. There are less than one hundred people left in Anvik.

Gone was the old *kashim*, the ceremonial bathhouse, where they danced the salmon dance to the drums, wearing masks, celebrating the coming of the fish, taking sweat baths. The *kashim* was built of logs caulked with moss and had a hard earth floor smoothed from the pressure of many feet. The men sat around a central fireplace on log benches blackened by smoke and grease and polished by bodies. Women were admitted only to bring meals and at festival time.

Women in those days used to throw the feathers of geese into rivers to be carried by the current, in the belief that they would become birds again and return to feed in their old haunts of mud and goose grass. They believed that fish bones would become fish if tossed into rivers. The bones of animals were taken back to the forest; they were not permitted to fall on paths where people passed, as it was thought that they would not become animals again.

The Ingaliks had a mask-making tradition, and I saw a porcupine mask made by Billy Williams, the oldest man at Anvik. The wooden base was covered with porcupine quills and in the center was a carved white face. The spirit of the mask was half man and half animal, for Ingaliks believed that animals shed their skins and became human at will. They said, "When we put on the masks, we are not ourselves."

Billy Williams sat at his cabin window watching me as he smoked a pipe. His cheekbones were curved like small apples and his eyes were opaque, almost sightless; he was an old man full of memories.

He had carved a berry-woman mask with black arched eyebrows over slanting eyes. The downcast mouth had three lines on the chin, and two blue trade beads resembling blueberries hung from her nose; bird feathers protruded from a willow frame around her nose.

When Billy was young there used to be wonderful mask dances. Dancing girls carried finger masks painted and ornamented with beads, feathers and white caribou hair. One dance representing the arrival of salmon depicted a woman carrying a fish attached to a stuffed loon. Two men representing sea gulls danced with her. I wish I could have seen it. The mask dances are still occasionally held in Grayling at Christmas time but not in Anvik anymore.

In addition to the dances, stories and myths were told in the *kashim* with imitation of animals, appropriate gestures and many bursts of laughter. The motions and exact words were memorized to be acted the same way every year.

Athabaskan stories reveal a strong interdependence among people, animals and the land. Frequently an animal helps man in time of need—a raven outsmarts the fox, a loon restores a blind man's sight or a mouse takes small stitches in a bark canoe to make it watertight.

The raven hero in folk tales epitomizes the desires of the people. If people could dominate the external world as completely as the raven does in the myths, then life would be more secure.

I was invited to vist the home of an older woman, a small grandmother in a black windbreaker and kerchief, whose neat home had wooden floors and blue printed curtains. She and her husband lived at a fish camp in the summer and trapped in the winter.

"We used to drink," she said, offering me a cup of tea, "but when I was in the hospital with TB, I made a promise to God: if I got over TB and lived, I'd never drink again, and I have never touched a drink since."

Rocking in her chair, she complained bitterly about the effects of welfare on families. "The children get money for candy and Coke, as the parents feel guilty because they drink. They never take care of their children and they get seven hundred dollars per month from welfare. I don't know where the money goes. They have nothing; they never work. What's going to become of all those young children, seeing their parents drunk all the time with nobody to teach them anything? They never save ahead, just use up all the money as soon as they can. They know welfare will give them more. It just ruins them."

Opening a trap door, she brought up three beautiful birch-bark baskets. "They were my mother's berry baskets and I will always keep them." I had never seen such intricate workmanship except in museums. Little birch-wood latches fastened the tops. The women were noted for their elaborate geometric designs on the edge of fur parkas, boot tops, wooden spoons and baskets. Animal tails, quills, feathers, shells and claws decorated fur garments.

In many ways, Anvik was like other villages I had seen all over the north. At nine o'clock the children sat at their school desks in a modern new building, the most expensive edifice they had ever seen. A child entered the antiseptic school, which smelled of crisp paper, books and ink, and was taught by teachers dressed in better clothing than she had ever seen. She tumbled out of bed, if she had a bed, and ate a meager breakfast, usually pilot bread and tea. In the winter she stumbled through snowdrifts in below-zero temperature, nose dripping, feeling the beginnings of the eternal cough and earache. She was susceptible to diseases of the lungs, especially tuberculosis and pneumonia, and to deafness due to running ears and nose.

At school children read books about other children whose fathers drove "cars" to "offices" but who never brought home food. The mother made "cookies" on a stove that had no flame, and when the children visited their grandparents, they saw strange, deformed animals, a "cow" and a "horse," which resembled a moose, and odd birds that didn't fly and were called "chickens."

In the school there was hot lunch. There was a noticeable difference in the summer, when school was out and no hot lunch was available; then children who were neglected suffered from malnutrition.

The children told me there had been a bear at the end of the village. They claimed that one boarded-up old house was "haunted." "I seen Dracula in the movies and I had bad dreams," said a seven-year-old boy. "Could he suck my blood?" I explained that there was no such person as Dracula, but I could see that they did not believe me; they believed the movie. Their grandparents had believed in legendary dreams, monsters and supernatural beings, and they were not to be dissuaded. Unfortunately, most of the old movies shown were violent ones or war pictures, and I dreaded the coming of television.

There was a monster legend about a place a few miles from the

Anvik River where it joined the Yukon. The people would not go by this place of monsters, preferring to portage their canoes around it, just beyond the mouth of the big slough.

They believed in bush men, or "Nakhani," who were evil spirits, half man and half animal, monsters who lurked around the camps and stole children and women. The Nakhani frightened children and were feared.

Before each potlatch or feast, a messenger wearing a miniature mask traveled to neighboring villages to invite the guests. They celebrated the death potlatch if someone died and the Feast of Animal Souls, the Feast of Dolls and the Feast of Masks.

They were once certain that the cause of sickness and misfortune was broken taboos. If a women was afraid to go into the woods to pick berries or roots, she would ask a shaman for a song. The song would turn the bear away, as he would know that the owner of the song was a friend. When the doctors and missionaries came, the people lost confidence in their shamans.

My friend Jean Dimenti, the first woman Episcopal priest in Alaska, told me that "when moon shots were made, before the landing the women worried because they heard on the radio that the moon was going to be shot. They had no concept how big the moon was or how far away, and to them it was important and they were worried. I told them how big the earth was and how far and large the moon was and that they were going to land on only one place. Then they were satisfied."

A tall white boy and a blond girl in an army parka told me they had a homestead eighty-three miles north of Anvik and that they had lived there for five months. They planned to winter there, with 250 pounds of flour, rice and other supplies. They had plenty of warm clothes and a snowmobile.

"Have you a moose yet?"

"Not yet," the boy replied. "I plan to trap, too."

The girl looked helpless, a city girl. At least they had a cabin, a rifle, an ax, a stove and plenty of wood. So many have starved or died from exposure.

Back on the barge, Dave spoke between cigarette puffs. "That white boy homesteading near here"—he paused—"he's on Indians' trap line."

"Why don't the Indians tell him?"

"Well, he got a homestead filing on it, legal."

I could imagine how they felt, a white man owning their trapping land legally. They could outwait the white man as they had always done. Discourage him. He would leave. Maybe.

Dave said that people were angry at that white man living on their trapping grounds, but they were quiet about it. I remember stories of white men shooting each other for such a thing in the early days when we first came to Alaska.

"Those old prospectors used to drink a lot, too, but no one ever holds it against them! Just let an Indian drink . . ." Dave did not finish the sentence.

I shook my head.

"Indians are good and they are bad, drink or not, same as everyone else," said Dave.

The children along the banks were badgering a baby muskrat they had found, but luckily it scampered back into the river. Two of the children led me between two rows of staked huskies and a stark-white Persian cat with long whiskers. Their small cabin had a low ceiling lined with cardboard. Laundry hung from the clothesline; beds were set in every available space.

The father, who had been a hunter, trapper and pilot on a stern-wheeler, lay paralyzed on the bed, having spent months suffering from a stroke in the Anchorage hospital. The family had ordered a wheel-chair about six months ago, but it had not yet come. All the medical help the father received now was from a "health aide," who dispensed aspirin and shots. The father was confined to a bed in the center of the

cabin. The family hauled water and used an outhouse. His wife had a heavy burden of several children to feed. Her hair hung limply around her careworn face as she lifted the blanket to cover her husband.

The young son told me about the bear he had shot and showed me a necklace of bear claws he had made. The other son, home from the service, was married to a blond girl with pigtails, the owner of the white cat.

Their cabin had the air of too many things compressed into a little space. The cluttered table held a large pot of fish stew. Living together in close quarters, the family was in danger of fire and tuberculosis. (A much-needed housing project was being built nearby.)

I soon had the children in the house, drawing with and sharing my paints. I bought the bear-claw necklace from the son, who walked me back to the barge, lighting the way with his flashlight.

The Episcopalian volunteer lay worker, a twenty-four-year-old geology graduate, had been in Anvik three weeks. He had cut lots of wood and shared his meals, sometimes with five or six children.

His quarters, belonging to the church, were elaborate compared to village standards. The young lay worker had much to learn. Unfortunately, ordained ministers were no longer being sent to villages, where little interest in the church was shown.

The first missionaries at Anvik were the Reverend Octavius Theodore Parker and his wife. A letter dated 1888, written by Mrs. Parker, told how they received permission to build on the Indians' land. They paid the Indians twenty skins, giving them what amounted to thirty yards of ticking, twenty cups of tea, twenty-five pounds of sugar and fifty pounds of flour. The Parkers refused to furnish the tobacco that the Indians wanted. "I told them that neither Mr. Parker nor I used it, and if we did, I thought it would make them unfit for work and asked them if they wanted such bad habits for their children." In return for the land the Parkers were to put up buildings and teach the children.

The Reverend John W. Chapman, the next Episcopal priest, learned the language. People still remembered him with respect. "Old Chapman," they said, "he sure could talk Indian good." They remembered Mrs. Chapman wearing long starched white dresses. Together the Chapmans saved many lives during the flu epidemic and worked hard for forty-three years, building a schoolhouse, a home, a sawmill and a church, dedicating their lives to teaching, praying and healing. Their son Henry also became a minister.

One depressing winter day, the reverend wrote in his diary: "I sometimes wonder whether I was destined to spend my life crawling these narrow tunnels on my hands and knees, choking in the smoky interiors . . . where disheveled creatures, hair uncombed, eyes bleared from smoke . . . sun . . . and . . . snow blindness . . . sucked their fingers after eating their meal of boiled fish, tucking away the remnants . . . under the wooden platform upon which they sat by day and slept by night."

A visit to the *kashim* gave him a start: "The room was so full of smoke that I could not see my companion and became alarmed."

He wrote of the housing conditions among the Indians: "A man put up a house just before winter . . . it was six feet high and ten feet square and looked like a mound of earth just about as high as my head . . . this hut is being occupied for the winter by ten people."

Chapman said that the dialect was the most fiendish one known to man. In order to say "Thank you," something like *"Noxwoquor-criqudastcet"* was required. Chapman advised that "you take out your larynx and scrape it, then you put it back after turning it inside out . . . then, placing the root of your tongue against the wisdom teeth and grasping a stove or anything solid, you breathe gently, and you have the word and sensation. It is a little hard at first, but after it is over, you feel all right." Chapman was of course exaggerating, but he did learn the language, which is more than I can say for myself.

CHAPTER 14

Holy Cross

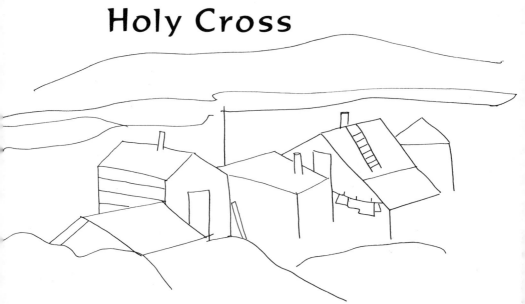

It is not easy to talk of the terror of this pestilence. The Indian life is very miserable even when they are in good health. Most of them live in tents in their summer villages and those that live in barabaros [primitive shelters] are not better off. They have no clothes and no proper food. A long parka-like sack is their dress during day and their blanket during night . . . their food is dry fish. But now their condition was such that one might say death was their relief.

You enter a tent and see a man and his wife and three or four children and some infant lying on a mat, all half naked, coughing up bile with blood, moaning, vomiting, passing blood with stools and urine, with purulent eruptions from eyes and nose, covered with oily, dirty rags, all helpless and wet day and night.

There were sixty-nine in this pitiful condition. Two fathers and a brother were bringing food and tea to them three times a day, and I was giving medicines. In this way we saved forty-one, who are now in good health. Father Peron was busy preparing them for a good and happy death and digging graves. Some died of the plague and others entirely exhausted by wasting disease, others of pneumonia, others of violent consumption, others of dysentery.

FATHER A. PARODI,
Jesuit House Journal, July 1900

I had seen Bishop Seghers' name on a slab of wood at the Nulato church and now I recalled the story that I read in the Jesuit journals in the University of Alaska archives. The Catholic mission on the Yukon was Bishop Seghers' dream. In 1886 he came to Alaska via the Chilkoot Pass, accompanied by Fathers Tosi and Robaut, both Jesuits, and Frank Fuller, a lay assistant. They wintered on the upper Yukon, planning to go in the spring to Nulato.

Fuller had acted in a peculiar manner, shooting a bear and pumping bullets into it long after it was dead. The men had been camping on the trail, within two days of Nulato, sleeping on a bearskin, when the deranged Fuller shot and killed the bishop.

Father Tosi carried on the bishop's work at Nulato, and Father Robaut began the mission at Holy Cross with the aid of the sisters of Saint Anne of Quebec. The thought of black-frocked Jesuits in a canoe going down the Yukon captivated me. Father Robaut gave his life to the mission, as did the sisters, all cut off from the rest of the world, martyrs in service. The sisters' trials began when they first arrived and their tent was overrun by mice; they prayed to be rid of them, only to find to their horror that when the mice left, they fled to the tent of the fathers.

I thought of the aging Father Robaut saving many orphans who would have died without his care during the plague. After years of service at Holy Cross, he was incapacitated with a stroke, painfully stuttering through mass.

The fathers had purchased a sawmill and built dormitories, a school and quarters for the sisters. A farm, cows, a vegetable garden and a small hospital were gradually added. Holy Cross became the garden spot of the Yukon.

The Jesuits were strict, expecting obedience and industry. Children were rapped on the knuckles for speaking their native tongue, wetting the bed and other infractions. After school they were kept busy working to sustain the mission.

The Indians had no immunity to white men's diseases, and in 1900 a devastating plague of flu, typhus, cholera and measles swept over Alaska. It was believed to have begun from a solitary case on a steamboat. Plague ran through the countryside, Indians dropped dead like flies and Holy Cross lost one-third of its population. Not a single canoe was seen on the river.

It was a heartbreaking story of a once healthy village. The tents contained dying families without food, too sick to care for one another. Starving children ate grass, like animals. The survivors were nursed, taken to the mission, bathed and fed, their dead carried to their graves by the Jesuits and nuns.

Father Parodi wrote of their horrible struggles:

We saw sights more dreadful than any yet encountered. Here and there bodies wrapped in skin mats and old garments laying about . . . one of them a little girl of ten who had been dragged by a rope around her neck, half-clothed, on muddy ground and left face downward . . . From another tent we took a body that gave forth a swarm of blue flies and worms when disturbed . . . from one of the bundles a long arm protruded in a ghastly way . . . the ground was strewn with all kinds of tools and cooking utensils, fishing tackle left behind by panic-stricken people . . .

We proceeded to bury the bodies . . . placing a large rude cross, hastily made.

Father brought a ten-year-old blind boy, ragged, barefooted, wet and famishing and lately orphaned by plague, a more wretched piece of humanity I have not seen. After a hot bath and general cleaning, he was put in a hot bed and dosed with hot beef tea . . .

Father Robaut and I went by bidarka up the Yukon to assist sick and bury the dead. The only living was a solitary dog who retreated into the village and curled himself up at the feet of his departed master.

The plague wrought havoc; the children were weakened and many developed tuberculosis. Father Alec Sipary noted in the house journal that the girls from the mission who later married died at an early age, for the sick and healthy lived together. He wrote:

Many consumptives are herded together. Dry fish and bread form their staple diet. The bread is wretched. The boys make it, mixed by hand. The boys are poorly clad in rags, washing done every two or three months. Bed sheets are not in use and blankets are never washed. You can imagine how we newcomers feel, crawling into blankets that have gathered their contributions from previous occupants, often greasy, not a bit attractive to nostrils.

A bread mixer was purchased and conditions gradually improved.

The plague, according to the journal, although a heavy scourge for natives, had a salutary effect on survivors. Indians saw how helpless the medicine men whom they used to trust were, and they turned to the Church. The Jesuits took over the role of protectors of the people, who confessed and received communion. Today instead of amulets, the people have rosaries or crucifixes. In the houses are little bottles of holy water, which are fed to ailing babies or rubbed on sore places.

Quoted below from the Jesuit house journal are some entries that give an idea of life in the twenties:

> May 11, 1921: Our boys return with 38 ducks, 12 geese, 2 swans, 2 cranes.
> May 12: All of the boys out of school bring into the shed about 100 cords of dry kitchen wood.
> July 9, 1921: First good run of dog salmon, about 750. Aloysius Vanda has a heavy hemorrhage of the lungs. He received last sacrament.

Other journal entries revealed the life at Holy Cross:

> December 24, 1920: Simon Kicik comes to take his adopted daughter home. The girl, however, refuses to go; upon which Simon goes and borrows money, sends a telegram to some high official in Fairbanks.
> December 25, 1920: Isabella Kicik makes out her affidavit before witnesses charging Simon K. with rape on her person. If the half insane gentleman persists in his demands the threat of a life sentence in the penitentiary will effectively stop him.
> December 28, 1920: That half crazy man Simon Kicik once more comes to get his adopted girl Isabella from the school. He is told to return with the marshall. He is reminded . . . he himself is likely to go off to penitentiary. Then he pretends he is going to take away his little boy Johnny. He is given permission to do so on condition he brings clothes to dress him up. He returns shortly, pretending he cannot find any at store, so he goes away.
> January 17, 1922: Mr. Frank Fox, who abducted Myrtle Atwate from her home last spring, is now here to pay her a visit. He is allowed an interview with her in presence of sister superior.
> February 3, 1922: Were it not for Aloysius Kicik, the dying boy who scarcely ever leaves the house, a fire would have resulted from blankets which the bed wetters squad had hung too close to the stove pipe.
> February 17, 1922: One of our junior boys caught in act of stealing from our dining room gets so overcome by grief . . . that he runs off towards the mouth of the Shageluk River . . . Returns soon . . . Father Ruppert starts the morning visit to baby house with a stick to cure bed wetting among the larger boys.
> June 11, 1922: Frank Fox, the "terrible turk," yielding to a personal invitation, pays a visit to Fathers' house . . . He [is] determined to let the girl go her way, and though persisting on making us respon-

sible for her change of affection, he left in a good mood. We all attribute the unexpected turn of affairs to our prayers.

Our barge came closer to Holy Cross. "We're nearing Bonasila Creek," Dave pointed out. "There used to be about twenty fishwheels and six houses here." He scanned the distance, eager to be home and see his family. "Been on the river while my kids are growing up.

"There used to be caribou, but ever since they put the railroad in, we never seen them." Dave said, navigating carefully. "It changed their way of traveling. Same thing will happen with the pipeline."

"Some people call the pipeline progress," I answered. "Some Alaskans call it progress when they bulldoze the wilderness and strip every tree and bush and then put up a shack, old cars and a collection of junk on it."

The geese circled overhead. About a hundred or more took off from the sand bar and flew east. "They'll come back. It's still too early for them to go south," remarked Dave, squinting as he turned the wheel.

Dave's knowledge of the Yukon was awesome. He could spot a bald eagle, a flock of swans or a bear faster than anyone I ever met. He could tell if it was a native or white man handling a small boat coming upriver from miles away. He knew how to read water, where the channels and sand bars were, even in the dark, it seemed. He was the first Indian pilot upgraded to officers' quarters and allowed to eat in the officers' mess instead of with deck hands.

The scenery became more spectacular; hills were higher and the gold-orange color was intensified after the rain. The sun sparkled on the water and the air was alive with ducks, geese and gulls. A net with buoys was set near the bluff, and the barge skirted away from it.

We came to a place named Walker's Slough, after Dave's father, James Walker, part Scottish, Russian and Indian, who was born in Old Station below Tanana. He settled in Holy Cross in 1890, chopping wood for the steamboats, piloting his own boat and hauling freight to the villages. He carried the mail to Iditarod, ran the store at Holy Cross for twenty years and transported freight until his death at eighty-seven. David inherited 365 patented acres from him.

I had read about James Walker in the old Jesuit journal. The fathers were against gambling and dancing and threatened that the Indians would not be allowed to build near the church property or to receive their sacraments if they did so.

"Things have indeed come to a pass that some of our young men

. . . no longer minded their parents . . . spend entire nights at James Walker's pool room, playing and gambling at cards . . ." The fathers partially solved the problem by installing their own billiard table.

When we docked, Dave's sons met him at the beach and shook hands formally. Dave invited me to hitch a ride in his jeep. He stopped to say hello to the schoolteachers Bill and Jeanne Browne. Without ceremony the Brownes invited me to stay at their trailer as long as I was in Holy Cross, as the boat was returning to Nenana in two days. Village people are always hospitable, but the Brownes were exceptionally so. They had taught in Alaska bush schools for seventeen years and loved their work. When they decided to bring their motorboat up from Nenana, Dave made a map for them from memory, showing every mountain, camp, bend and point in the river.

I walked down the dirt trail past barking dogs. Curtains moved back, for everyone in town knew the boat had landed and that I was a new face. A woman stuck her head out of the window and invited me in. Her name was Oxenia. "Not much rain this summer," she said. "All berries dried up. Even the rose hips little bitty things." At Holy Cross the old people did not pick greens anymore. "We buy them canned."

As I walked on, a woman in a blue parka invited me into her log house. Pansies grew in her window box, and she had a potato patch, the roots' leaves still green, although it was late autumn.

"The wind really howls around here," she remarked, holding the door open. "Are you Mrs. Art, the captain's wife?" Frances Demientieff inquired.

I was not, but she invited me in anyway. The table was set for tea, with cloth and teapot. Framed photos of the family, a picture of Jesus and plates hung on the wall. A friend, Rose Cristo, was seated on a cretonned couch surrounded by pillows and geranium plants. We had tea with homemade bread and salmon strips.

To our mutual enjoyment, I found that Rose Cristo had lived in Flat, where Joe and I had lived thirty years before, at the Keturis' gold mine. She knew Johnny Stevens and Olaf Olsen, the old miners who had worked there. "Well, you're one of us," she said, "not a cheechako or tourist."

They told me that the geese and cranes had been flying over the village by the thousands the past three days. The flock we had seen early yesterday was of emperors. Mrs. Demientieff waved her hand. "They fly over and it looks like they're writing letters to us in the sky."

Mrs. Demientieff showed me her skin-and-bead moccasins, her parka trim and an altar cloth of beaded moose hide. She had a basket-

ful of old beads and was kept busy with orders. Indian women who
know the art of beadwork or basketry can earn extra money as long as
they are willing to work arduous hours in dim light, threading small
beads.

When I left it was raining. Mist rose from the river; the yellow
birches seemed dulled, as if frost had struck. Back on the boat I asked
if Ray, the engineer, and his brother had returned from their hunting
trip. "They got back," answered the deck hand with emphasis on
"back." Later Ray told me he had seen moose tracks. "Lots of geese,
but we didn't have a shotgun. Geese were slopping around in the
mud." He added sheepishly, "We didn't get a thing."

Dave pointed to Betty Johnson, who with her husband was building a new grocery store at Holy Cross. "Take her with you, Ray, next time you go hunting. She gets her moose in forty below." Betty had come aboard to check off her grocery order and stayed to have coffee with us. Dave told us how she and her nephew went out with her snowmobile, "a little way out of town, by Deadman's Slough. Left at one and returned with a moose, butchered and on a sled by seven-thirty."

Betty, attractive in her red hat and windbreaker, told us that at fourteen she was a cook on a small houseboat. "The trader on it was big and fat. I dished up this big platter of moose meat and offered it to him. He fell over dead. Some shock I had. The other men aboard left me alone with him to get help. I was scared stiff." Betty delicately put down her coffee cup.

It was the last coffee I shared with the Petersons and the crew before the boat returned to Nenana. I had become part of the boat family. I kissed Adriana and Captain Art and the others aboard. I hated to part, but I wanted to stay longer. I had finally become oblivious to the noise of the motors; the boat had sheltered me well and brought me safely to shore. I moved my duffel bag and paintbox over the Brownes' trailer, offering to pay them per diem, but Bill waved the money aside, so I volunteered to take over his class and give an art lesson.

I walked away from the village into the woods down the muddy trail in my rough boots, a kerchief covering my head, hands stuck into my pockets. I felt free and happy to be here doing the work I love.

I trod deeper and deeper into the leaves and silence. Grasses waved, breezes rippled through the leaves and multitudes of insects kept up a ceaseless hum. Yellow birch leaves surrounded me, traced against the brown earth and blue sky.

The forest was illuminated by sunshine, and mosses were wet and soft against tree bark. The flying gnats and bees wove back and forth, adding music and aliveness to the scene. Cranberries grew in wine-red clumps near the rotted stumps; the odor was wild and rank. Insect territory.

I breathed deeply of mingled river scents, listening to the lapping of the water and to geese honking. I could sense what this land meant to people who had been born here. They felt it in every bone and fiber of their being; when they left it, they yearned to be back. I walked back, refreshed in my whole being, filled with joy.

"Joy is the most infallible sign of the presence of God," wrote Teilhard de Chardin, the Jesuit. He would have loved Holy Cross. "Throughout my life," he wrote, "by means of my life, the world has little by little caught fire in my sight, until, aflame all around me, it has become almost completely luminous from within."

I climbed to the top of the hill. The sun shone on the golden forest, illuminating the hills; Holy Cross houses were gathering in the last rays. Rosy-cheeked village children ran laughing down the hill, dogs chasing them. Red pants flapped on a line in the wind.

Nick and Belle Demientieff were unloading their boat, dragging boxes up on the beach, when I met them. They had returned to Holy Cross to live out their old age after thirty-one years in Fairbanks.

I had heard the name Demientieff ever since I had come to Alaska; the name is synonymous with the history of Alaska and the Yukon. The Demientieffs have built boats, freighted and fished the Yukon for years. Nick, a dark man with strong shoulders and a powerful chin, invited me into their log house.

Belle warmed her hands near the coffeepot, her back against the

rusty old Lang stove, which was just beginning to heat the cabin. Her slight frame held a lively spirit.

"The windows were all broken when we were gone." Nick motioned toward a pile of tools and lumber. "We have lots of work to do before winter."

Groceries and belongings were still in the packing boxes stacked against the flood-stained walls. In their hospitable way they invited me to sit down "in the chair that had come all the way from Iditarod."

Nick settled back and reminisced: "My grandfather was sent to buy furs in Kuskowim. Eskimos came to meet the boat, and when [the people on the boat] saw them, they thought they were going to attack. The ship left in a hurry, leaving my grandfather on shore. He settled on the Kuskowim, marrying an Aleutian woman. They had five boys and three girls. When his parents died, the Catholic Church picked up the boys and brought them here to Holy Cross. They were the boys who helped build this mission. They trapped, hunted and fished for the church. My dad married an Anvik girl. I saw him get ten thousand dog salmon one year for the mission. We used to get up at five every day to go fishing."

"We had ten kids," volunteered Belle. "Raised them on our boat." One son died in a plane crash.

Nick described their return to the Yukon: "On the way to Holy Cross we came to an old slough. Our boat had a kicker and little cabin on it, and we planned to spend the night. We watched muskrats and beaver swimming around a big cottonwood tree. It got dark; we slept on the floor. Got up at three, made coffee and breakfast. At daylight I heard the first hawk, then geese, then camp robbers and a blackbird. I poked along the beach looking for moose tracks, saw a grizzly. The camp robber followed me and flapped his wings. I said to my wife, 'I never in my life!' Seems like he was happy I come back to camp there.

"I called a moose with my horn, heard sticks break; the brush went *chrrrrrrr* and there was a moose." The Demientieffs got their moose before they reached Holy Cross—a good omen for them.

I asked if there were many changes since they had come back. Belle interrupted Nick and motioned with her hand: "There's a lake near here. We used to swim, but now there's a lot of garbage in it." She poured me a strong cup of coffee.

"I was trapping in Iditarod in the fall, living in a tent, driving dogs, when the river froze over," Nick said. "It snowed, covering the open place on the winter trail. There were two of us, with a dog team—I was on handlebars and my partner was in the sled. I jumped to one side.

"Went into ice up to my shoulders and got out hanging by my nails. I was soaking wet. Went down to Charlie Housner, from Flat. He lent me his union suit and I wrapped it around me twice, then he brought out his biggest size—forty-eight—pants and made a big V in the behind."

On a more sober note, Nick worried: "What are our children's children going to hunt? Will it be like the lower forty-eight? Are the moose going the way of the buffalo?" Great resentment was building up in all the villages against the white trophy hunters who came in floatplanes killing moose, taking only the rack and leaving the meat. It made the Indian hunters feel full of anxiety. They knew the moose population was down and the game regulations were getting tougher for subsistence hunters. Nick's butchered moosehead was in his shed; the vacant eyes followed me when I left.

I passed an old man digging up turnips and carrots from his garden. He could have been a model for a Millet painting. "Frost is sure to come tonight," he said, straightening up. He was digging the same spot the mission garden used to be on fifty-four years ago. "The girls of the mission," the house journal read, "were set to work spooning the cutworms and maggots from the cabbages."

After years of church-planted gardens, there was little evidence that they had taken hold in any big way, mainly because gardens were too weakly rooted in Indian culture. Indians preferred moose to vegetables.

As I sat on the beach sketching an old wooden hull, two girls walked by, blowing violet bubbles as big as their faces. They asked shyly if I was the artist. Soon they were draped around, watching me paint.

"At fish camp we had no sweets or gum, no candy all summer," the girl in the red sweater complained. She scrutinized my painting. "I chewed the same gum for two weeks or more." I confessed to them that when I was a child we were so poor that I saved my bubble gum overnight.

It began to drizzle, pitting the Yukon. "We would go swimming every day," said the other girl.

"Isn't the Yukon too cold?" I asked.

"No, we built a big fire and warmed up afterward."

The girls had helped their folks cut salmon strips all summer. They said that they were eagerly waiting for me to come to school, as they had never had art lessons before. My painting was beginning to get water spots where I did not want them. When the rain washed all the color out, I had to stop.

Whymper, the artist, wrote that he had a hard time painting in the winter on the Yukon. "Between every five strokes of the pencil I ran about to exercise myself, or went to our quarters for warmth. Several times I skinned my fingers, once froze my left ear, which swelled up nearly to the top of my head, and I was always afraid that my prominent nasal organ would get bitten . . ."

I considered myself lucky. The coldest spot I ever painted was in Point Hope, an Eskimo village. I stood painting in two feet of snow, dressed warmly in underwear, parka, mukluks and gloves. Before the paint reached my block of paper, it was covered with a skin of ice. The eventual watercolor of the arctic house, the fastest I ever painted, was purchased by the West Point Museum.

True to my word, I brought my oil box into the classroom and gave an exhibition of my paintings. I talked to the children, encouraging them to paint, dipping my brushes in the bright oil colors and painting a portrait of one of the students. The children were fascinated and asked questions. The student I had selected to paint was one of the Demientieff girls. Her mother, Mary D., as she was affectionately called by the Brownes, was the school cook. Holy Cross seemed as full of Demientieffs as Minto was of Tituses.

I had lunch at the schoolhouse with the Brownes and Dave Walker's mother, an agile eighty-year-old, who was on the school board. Dave had taken me to her house and introduced us. For her birthday, her grandchildren gave her a snowmachine! Acting as midwife, she had delivered all of her grandchildren.

"It's Friday and there's ham," she said disapprovingly, as a good Catholic. Delicious scalloped potatoes, homemade bread and apple pie that Mary D. had baked were set before us, and I needed no coaxing.

"We used to be very particular about food," Mrs. Walker said, "not to throw it on the floor or step over it, because they say that someday you might be hungry, and if you don't waste food, the One that takes care of us above will see that you don't get hungry. I wish young people would know that. They think nothing of wasting food.

"Those old people had no stores, yet they had everything! They had furs and bird skins. You know they made clothes with them, even down to the muskrat tail. They used to make thread out of that little sinew right on the tail. Yes, about six inches. Sinew." Their needles were made of bird wings.

"When white people need something, they go to the bank to get money, and us, when we need something, we go to our land and that's our bank. People cared for the land and the animals and the children. They had to take care of everything. Oh, they loved their land. Their life, that land."

I visited Mary D. in her cosy log cabin, the home of ten children, who used every nook and corner of it. Her husband, Joe, worked as a carpenter. The cabin was filled with the scent of ten loaves of rising bread and fish soup simmering on the back of the stove. Children came and went quietly, and Steff, the Browne's son, sat reading in a corner.

"I went to the Holy Cross mission school," Mary D. said, punching down the bread dough with her fists, her braids swinging over her little earrings. "It was hard, but I learned everything in it. If not for it, I don't know what I'd be doing. The girls used to wear aprons over long dresses, and buttoned shoes. We had three aprons—one for good, one for best and one for work."

She baked bread for her family every other day and for the school every day, and she handled the bread as if it were the simplest thing in the world. I admired her ease, as I baked bread and could appreciate how good she was at it.

"I used to pluck thirty ducks at a time, and with two kids in diapers always. I had one kid a year except one year—I had a miscarriage. I'm forty-one now. I don't know how I did it, but the kids were always good, no trouble—they're healthy. I had five at fish camp and the rest at the hospital," she said cheerfully, placing the loaves in the hot oven. Her daughters had inherited her smile and serene inner spirit, truly a great gift. One of her daughters complained, jokingly, that Mom was always cheerful, even when the others felt crabby.

Mary D.'s father, Dahlquist, was known for running the diphtheria serum in relays with Leonard Seppala on that fateful dog-team trip from Nome.

The bread filled the cabin with its aroma and, when done, was crusty and flavorful; we ate it slathered with butter. Jeanne was also baking bread at the Brownes' trailer house, while Bill, her husband, turned the ice cream freezer for the school sale tomorrow. Steff, their son, fed a baby weasel slivers of moose meat. It was curled up in his palm, begging to be sketched. (At Grandma Demientieff's I had tasted *naltloda*, Indian ice cream made with beaten tallow, fish flakes, sugar and berries, a real treat.)

In the morning I heard Bill shoveling dirt. He was building a sauna and bathhouse in back of their trailer. It reminded him of a story about

Marshall, a neighboring village, where they used to teach. The Eskimo women, who were usually shy, had burned down the men's bathhouse. No one would tell the reason for this uprising.

Holy Cross is the borderline between the Eskimos and the Indians on the Yukon, the two existing side by side but with different cultures. There is intermarriage. In one of the homes I visited, an unmarried Indian mother held a newborn baby. The father was an Eskimo, so they nicknamed the baby "Indeskimo." The baby was picked up constantly and petted by everyone in the family. Birth control or any sexual behavior outside of marriage was frowned upon by the Catholic Church.

The Brownes felt that the Eskimos at Marshall had a strong sense of community: they had retained their own language, festival days, hunting traditions and dog races. At Holy Cross there were no Indian dances, and few spoke Indian anymore. "They lost their language and their dances," Bill said, throwing out a shovelful of dirt.

Dancing was the cause of much trouble at Holy Cross, according to the Jesuit journal of February 2, 1921:

> Our people are being carried away by an insane craving for white man's dance. The Ghost Creek outfit, James Walker . . . is giving dances every few days.

January 16, 1921:

> All women made the promise before the sacrament to abstain from "white man" dances. The men are indignant and come in a body to ask that the women be released from their promise, which they say infringes on their obedience due to their husbands . . . It was well explained to them that this was no *vow*, that they should act with absolute freedom, out of a drive to please God . . . and to safeguard their families . . . that the sisters who had educated and trained those women in their girlhood had the right to advise them and that they knew perfectly well what was proper and what was not in a Christian woman. Tongues were virulent the rest of the day in the village.

On New Year's Day at fifty-one below:

> People of the village gave the sisters an exhibition of Indian dancing. Truly most innocent and much less reprehensible than the dances in vogue among the whites.

This dance may have been accepted, but ceremonial dances were considered pagan, danced out of fear to appease animalistic spirits.

Widow Anna Frank, who had never heard of the Anne Frank who died in a concentration camp in Germany, was born in 1914, at the beginning of World War I.

Anna looked mournful, a *mater dolorosa*, weighed down with troubles, her hair in a long braid. Her expression was soft and kindly, but without humor or vigor. "I'm tired, I have arthritis. Can't pick berries," she said sorrowfully. "I brought up four kids and worked hard. One son is in the Methodist University."

She told me of her youth: "My dad died when I was thirteen, so my mother raised us by sewing. My brothers trapped and sawed wood for the steamboats, and I went to the mission school.

"When I first came here as a girl, this place was all bare, no trees. The mission had fresh milk; they kept cows and goats. Gardens everywhere. Now there are trees everywhere and no cows."

Now she lives in new housing, with three bedrooms, running water, a large freezer and other conveniences, for only sixteen dollars a month.

The temperature dropped to forty degrees and it was cold at night. The stars were brilliant; yellow leaves on muddy roads hardened with the frost. After a Sunday breakfast with the Brownes of baked apples, bacon, onion-and-egg omelet and oatmeal bread, I painted one of the little girls who came to visit. Every time I said something the girls liked, they exclaimed in unison, "Holy, holy, holy," like angels singing.

Father Dan, the Catholic priest, was getting ready to take a trip when I dropped in to visit the sisters. They were baking pans of cinnamon buns and moose roast in their large kitchen. Their work took them to the surrounding villages, where they taught the catechism. A sister superior had died during the cholera epidemic from the strain of overwork. A story written in the journal by Father Parodi told about the sisters' treatment of the sick children with coal oil and whiskey. They had no other knowledge of how to treat the plague at that time.

Father Parodi wrote: "They had heard that flour and water cured diarrhea, so they gave flour and water. In this way nine girls died. I was told to give coal oil and carbolic acid to the boys. I did so for one day, that if any boy would die, they might not accuse me of letting him die without coal oil. One day I saw the man who was curing everybody with coal oil and I told him we were not successful.

"He said, 'In what way did you give it?'

" 'Well, I put a few drops in a spoon and I gave it to them to drink.' "

" 'Oh,' he explained, 'That is not the way; you must give it in capsules!' If I understand well, it is not the coal oil that cures, it's the capsule," wrote Father Parodi.

Father Dan, the sisters and I talked about art and religion at Holy Cross. They felt that the Indians had too hard a life to have developed much art. The Tlinget Indians always had an artist in their midst, but I had never heard of an Athabaskan artist in the early days. The Tlingets had a warmer climate and abundant food, which gave them leisure to develop their totemic art. Here, though, I could not find a single basket for sale, although I inquired everywhere. Perhaps in the winter the women had more leisure time.

White crosses covered the hillsides, yet Father Dan did not think that the church had made a dent. "Just a drop in the bucket. It will take one hundred years," he said. He felt that the stick dance was pagan, yet the Brownes and Mary D., who taught catechism, all good Catholics, said it was a meaningful, beautiful custom to mourn the dead.

Mary D. drove Father Dan, the sisters and me to the airport. Mary D. seemed to be wherever in the village there was a need. "In the old days we were supposed to be seen but not heard," she laughed, "but I'm seen and heard." Bill Browne quipped, "She's airport liaison officer, too." What a woman she was!

The mission taught the Indians much and provided many needed services. But I could not help feeling that the people had yet to become responsible for their own destinies. In spite of its good works, the Church tended to become overprotective, like mothers who did not trust the judgment or believe in the strength of their adult children.

PART II

CHAPTER 15

Nenana

Fill up my jingling cup with tea.
Now won't you let us alone, please.
Come and join the Indian dance.
We don't want the white man's dance.

POTLATCH SONG,
collected by Wallace Olsen

A year after my trip to Holy Cross, I boarded *The Tanana*, sister ship to *The Yukon*, in Nenana. We would be traveling in the direction opposite last year's trip, going up the Yukon toward the Canadian border. It was Captain Brown instead of Peterson who greeted me. A river pilot of thirty-five years, Brown had the reputation of being "strict." He looked level-eyed at me and laid down the rules: "I don't allow the crew in the pilothouse. No drinking on board except in your own room, and men and women keep separate." Then he added, "You are invited up to the pilothouse anytime." I promised to keep out of his way and thanked him.

We had four hours before sailing, so I decided to visit Susy Boatman, one of Nenana's oldest residents. The bushes, trees, wildflowers and weeds were full of bees, and there was a hazy, lazy air about Nenana. Down a dirt road was Susy's house, plywood shoe-box style with one room for an old lady. She greeted me by saying, "I'm the only one left of the real people," as she shoved a fly from her arm.

Prominent cheekbones and wide nostrils gave her a look of alarm. Her narrowed eyes were wary of me, a stranger, when I stated, "I'm an artist." Her wrinkled face, especially her upper lip, deepened as she led me indoors.

Her small Yukon stove, which kept her warm all winter, had the usual basin, pot and teakettle on it. Bloody chunks and strips of fresh moose meat dripped onto a piece of cardboard. Flies buzzed.

"Nenana used to be the biggest village around here. Lots of hunting and trapping. People came from all over for potlatches." Susy

pushed aside a can of sweet cherries she had been eating. "I was an orphan. My mother died when I was a baby, so the mission brought me up.

"The people helped Bishop Rowe build the mission for no pay," said Susy. "When the railroad came, Bishop Rowe told the railroad people, 'They are my people. They will do what I tell them.' They bulldozed our cabins along the river to make way for the tracks and they dug up our old graves." After the railroad came, white people moved to Nenana, bringing flu and creating widows and orphans. (One-fourth of Nenana Indians died.) Indians then moved to Minto, as white people were encroaching on their land, spreading their conflicting customs and diseases.

Nenana Indians, as well as the Minto people, married into the Caribou or Fishtail clans. The old people used to hang fishtails on their doors to ward off death, but there were no fishtails on Susy's door.

"I'm too sick now to go anyplace," said Susy, hushing her dog. "Glad you came to visit me. I had typhoid fever and pneumonia three times." I mentioned that I had lived with Charlotte Adams of Beaver. Then the wary look in her eyes disappeared, and she smiled. "She's a saint. She took care of me in hospital. Brought me Native food."

"People give me blueberries and meat," she said later, "and I get social security. Gladys Coghill remembers me. We helped them when they first came here."

The Coghill family opened their store in 1917, selling everything from rifles and liquor to groceries, often giving credit to people in need. In addition to Coghill's there was Fowler's, the old trading store. According to a story I heard from Charley Purvis, who lived in Nenana, Chief Alexander used to trade there.

Sometimes when the chief would drink with his friends, his wife would wait up for him at night, afraid he would perish in a snowdrift on his way home. One winter day when the chief woke up, his stove was out and he had no food or wood in the cabin. He found an old shoe pack and put it in the stove to burn. He had worked hard all summer as a riverboat pilot. "I spent all my pay on booze! I'm going to quit," he said. He put on his jacket and went down to Fowler's.

"How much I owe you?" he asked.

"Two hundred fifty dollars," said Fowler. The Indians were never out of debt to him.

"I'm not going to pay you one cent," said the chief. "I work all year and haven't got a cent left and I'm still owing you money." The chief went out, sobered up and never touched another drop. He began to trade with Coghill's. Fowler's never dunned him.

Chief Alexander used to say, "I was raised on rotten fish heads. I like them, but don't you give me any of your Limburger cheese."

"I buried eleven children," said Susy, smoothing her hair down. "Only one son still living." Susy's husband was a white railroad worker called Old Boatman, fifty years her elder. She must have had an iron constitution to have lived through the miseries of her children's death. Breech deliveries were difficult and babies usually suffocated. Some women hemorrhaged to death or died from infections.

The suffering of children was great in those days. The infant mortality rate in Alaska was twice that of the national average, and in 1950, 95 percent of the children were affected by tuberculosis by the age of fourteen. Happily, the disease has been controlled since, but I remember my trips to the Arctic in the late fifties and the worry I had of contacting TB.

"There isn't a movie and no place to go except the bars," said Susy, sitting down in her stuffed chair. Actually, there is bingo and Native doings at George Hall, and the Civic Center has a celebration at ice-breakup time. When we first came to Fairbanks in 1946, the Nenana River ice-breakup lottery was the most exciting event in the spring after a long dreary winter. Alaskans bet thousands of dollars on the exact day and minute the frozen ice would break up. Nenana could count on yearly employment because of the ice pool. Susy had never been lucky enough to win the lottery.

When we parted she told me to give her love to Charlotte Adams of Beaver.

When I boarded *The Tanana,* dense fog had settled on the river, so we waited out the night until the morning sun burned it away. Clear skies and a glint of sun through my window the next morning revealed an idyllic day to begin.

The next day, the weather changed suddenly. One of the sand bags loosened by the wind almost hit the captain, causing cables to fly through the air. The captain and I watched the Indian deck hands working, tying down the billowy tarps and climbing over the tops of oil drums.

The captain surveyed the river and spoke through his pipe. "There was a young couple who lived thirty-five miles from Stevens Village," he said, puffing. "I had some grub to drop off, but when I stopped at the bank no one was home. I didn't want to leave it out on account of bears. The woman had given birth out there herself. The mosquitoes were just terrible. She came out to get groceries with the baby, as her husband was working in Fairbanks. I told her, 'You shouldn't stay here by yourself,' and I offered her a lift to Stevens Village, where she could stay. 'Oh, I'm all right long as I have something to eat,' she said.

"Then in fall I dropped off a snowmobile for them. Then I heard that that winter she wanted to go to Stevens Village and had started out alone on the snow machine. The machine broke down two miles from Stevens, and instead of walking to Stevens, she tried to follow her tracks back to the cabin. They found her frozen body close to the house. Only a few miles!"

I awoke to a chill cold wind smashing against the window. The tarps were puffed up with wind and treetops swayed, the water ruffled and gold sun blasted everything. I huddled under the blankets, trying to stay warm, then forced myself to get up and wash my hair. There was a full yellow moon last night, and when seen behind the spruce it looked like a Canadian whiskey advertisement for northern forests.

The sounding boat bounced in the water churning with two-foot waves. Frost had nibbled the green out of trees and turned the grasses wheaten. The Yukon was silver mud, and each wave peaked and toppled with white froth. I missed the passing of *The Yukon* going downstream. The Petersons blew the whistle and waved, I learned, but I was sound asleep on my bunk.

One of the deck hands needed surgery and had to leave the boat; his finger had been broken in an Indian finger-wrestling game!

Mary, the cook on *The Tanana,* presided over her black stove, talking about engine vibrations as she clumped about in her heavy boots without stockings: "I love the sound of motors, it puts me to sleep at night." Owlish glasses sat on the bridge of her nose and she smoked incessantly, hopping about like a young chicken. "I like to be around young kids. I tried living with a woman of my age, but I couldn't stand it." She chopped enthusiastically, demolishing two onions, wiping her hands on a mottled towel around her waist. "I'm too busy to sit around." In the winter she cared for the Catholic priests. In earlier days she would have crossed the Chilkoot Pass in her staunch boots, nursing sourdough batter in her backpack and cheering on the weary and footsore pilgrims.

The boat crawled slowly up the Yukon about four miles an hour against strong currents; the radio reported a thirty-five-mile gale. Dust rolled off the sand bars, resembling fog, and when I walked on deck, wind smacked my clothes.

The engineer came out from his dungeon and nodded at the waves: "This is the worst I've seen." He gulped his black coffee and disappeared down the lower depths.

Captain Brown looked thoughtfully at the colorless sky. "Season is too short. Don't want the boats to get frozen in, it's too costly." He stood sure-footed at the wheel, pipe in mouth, a Dick Tracy of the river detecting the shallow spots by osmosis.

Rampart Canyon acted as a funnel, eventually forcing us to tie up against the storm. On the wind came a rich humus smell of autumn. The captain and two deck hands went ashore to look for signs of bear and moose when we tied up.

In the evening a pink-orange sunset rose, outlining the spruces on the steep hillsides. "This river can turn to ice overnight," Captain said as he filled his pipe, his face tranquil. His expression betrayed no struggle. Did he keep orderly thoughts in calm procession? His inner clock seemed to move ahead, ticking correct time. It was contagious and I felt myself shifting to "river time." It had been a strange day, the boat captive on the river, unable to move. The river was somber in a wasteland of sere stubble and bent trees, and I wondered why in this oppressive place I felt so full of well-being, striding around the dark deck, grateful to be here.

CHAPTER 16

Rampart

*Minook's child was too sick for white man's medicine. The shaman
was called about midnight to begin his incantations . . . the shaman
was groaning, yelling and indulging in all sorts of contortions, all
the while keeping time with his noises and kicks to the spasmodic
singing of the surrounding group. At one corner of the canvas Minook,
with his child in his arms, was sitting. After writhing and
groaning under the blanket for an hour or more, the shaman thrust
his feet into Minook's lap, under the wraps of the child. He lay
in that position for some time, then he broke away with the
disease of the child in his possession. He began a terrible struggle
with the disease in order to drive it back into the keeping of the evil
spirit. During this contest he tore his shirt from his body, floundered
to the top of the blanket and seemed to suffer the most excruciating
pains. At the end of two hours, when his exertions had become less
violent, one of the natives seized him, drew his head into his lap,
blew into an ear.*

LIEUTENANT HENRY T. ALLEN,
Reconnaissance in Alaska, 1887

AT four in the morning there was
a knock on the door: "We're coming to rapids!" Peering out in the
early morning fog, I saw tree-studded hillsides, canyons with huge
rocks jutting out of the water. I stumbled into my shoes and ran out,
buttoning up. The boat veered to the left as we bypassed the rocks.

Lieutenant Frederick Schwatka, the explorer, compared the rapids
to the "stupendous grandeur of the Yosemite or Yellowstone Rivers."
No white water was visible—just low water and a fog obscuring the

view of the "stupendous grandeur." I was disappointed after all I had
been led to believe.

My husband, Joe, who had mined gold in Rampart in 1950, always
spoke of the beauty of this canyon. He had leased old Pete Larkin's
gold claim off Big Minook River, but the ground turned out to yield
nothing. Big Minook River was named after Minook, a Russian Indian
from Nulato, who prospected there. Rampart was full of mined-out
ground; few had struck it rich. Old-timer Harry Havrilick, who used to
be called "the Hollywood kid" because of his natty mustache, mined
at our old claim now and occasionally showed us some nuggets.

We passed an eagle's nest on top of a spruce twisting in a restless
sky. The river's changing color was a constant source of amazement
as we plodded along—it had now turned from silver silt to green ocher.

Rampart, only eighty miles from Fairbanks, was founded by Captain Mayo and Leroy McQuesten. Once it was a booming mining
center with its own newspaper. In 1898 there were 450 cabins, 10
stores, 12 saloons, 1 brewery, 6 restaurants and a hospital. The population at its height had been about 3,000 white people. The gold-camp
residents had been a restless bunch who followed each new gold strike.
Most of them unloaded their claims at a profit to newcomers and left
for the beaches of Nome, as did Rex Beach, who wrote *The Spoilers.*

According to Judge Ballou, who became ill with scurvy from eating a miner's diet, "There have been three fatal shootings since I
arrived, so we have had a dead man for breakfast most every morning . . . there were also heart attacks and suicides, and seven men froze
to death on the trail."

The old cabins of Rampart sat among the gold foliage, their backs
against the green hills. Sun glinted on the tin roofs and logs when we
tied up at noontime. Now that most of the prospectors had left, Rampart was quiet again. No plastic or smog. The air smelled clean and it
felt safe in a way a city could never feel. I doubted if anyone bothered
to lock his door.

I poked my head into the large cavernous interior of Weisner's
store, sniffing the acrid smoke from the barrel stove. A berry scent
pervaded the low ceiling, the old desk, the pool table and the ancient
canned goods.

Weisner, the white trader, was maneuvering a bulldozer to bring
up his oil drums and groceries. I had read his periodic ads for help in
the Fairbanks *News-Miner*: "Cook and housekeeper wanted, blonde
preferred, to help at the Rampart Trading Post." Weisner had originally traveled to Rampart by dog team and there he spent his life. He

set up a lumber mill and tried to can salmon commercially with Indian help.

Rampart was originally a white man's town built on the south side of the Yukon. (Indians built on the north side, where the sun shines longer.) The village is now occupied by five Indian families and Weisner. There are only twelve children in the school at present.

Poldine Carlos and her husband had built a new log cabin in the village, which they occupied in the summer, when they flew in from Fairbanks to work their mine and fish for salmon.

Nearby smoke curled out of an older cabin belonging to Mrs. Wood, the village's midwife and healer. Inside, she and Mrs. Evans were drinking tea. At eighty, Mrs. Wood had luxuriant gray hair and the step of a woman half her age. "I'm related to almost everyone in the village," she said. Called "Auntie," she had delivered about seventy-one babies at the last count—a woman to depend upon—and she herself had given birth to five children, cutting her own cord from the last child.

Her square stove was an old Volunteer model and she filled her teakettle with drinking water from a creek two miles away. We drank tea and watched a dozen crows and a coyote feeding on fish heads on the sand bar across the river.

The village might be old and poor, but it had a dignity and beauty. People had left for the larger cities, and some traveled back and forth. Maybe living near the river and savoring things slowly, not pushing time or the river, did prolong life. I felt at peace with myself as I sat in the kitchen. I invited the women to visit me in Fairbanks and left for the boat.

The captain picked up a river hitch-hiker, an old-timer named Frank Reinoski, with deep-blue eyes and a gray beard, who was going to cut his winter wood twenty miles upriver. He wore a battered felt hat and muddy pants with holes, and out of his denim jacket a small dog poked his head.

Frank had lived in Alaska for sixty-four years. No Pioneer Home for the elderly for him; he would rather take his chances in the woods. "When he was younger he could live on land that a wolf could starve to death on," the trapper Fabian Carey had said with respect. "He was the oldest trapper on the Yukon. One of the toughest men I ever knew."

Frank knew the country and had learned Indian ways. If he lost his matches, he could start a fire with flint, striking sparks into birch fungus. He knew how to keep warm even in forty below, piling high logs that would hold a fire all night. In the rain, spruce branches sheltered him and spruce boughs made a good bed. In an emergency he could wrap himself in fresh moose hide dried in front of a fire.

This time of year cranberries grew in the wet sphagnum, Labrador tea leaves were abundant and wild rhubarb and celery grew everywhere for the taking. Even the inner fiber of willow bark could be used as emergency food.

"The red on the hillsides is low-grade iron ore," Frank pointed out while I did a watercolor of him and his sleeping mongrel. "This tiny dog has had six litters," he said, stroking her head. "She chased a bear. A real fighter."

According to Joe, my husband, who met Frank when he mined there, Frank's cabin had a worn path from stove to bunk to table, with books piled several feet high everywhere. The curious thing about Frank was that he had dug a tunnel about one hundred eighty feet, to uncover a meteorite he believed was buried there despite all opinion to the contrary. I wondered why, at his age, he was so absorbed in digging. It did seem strange, but it gave him exercise in the coldest months and a purpose to his life. At eighty-five he did without doctors, cutting his own wood, shooting his own meat and planting his own garden.

About twenty miles from Rampart, the captain lowered the ramp for Reinoski and his dog. We watched his small figure carrying his meager belongings fade into the sloping wilderness. I yelled from the boat, "Good luck, Frank." He was going to cut wood, then raft it back to Rampart. His entire outfit consisted of a box with handles and two wheels, no gun. The small box contained some grub, a saw and ax. I could see no blanket or bedroll. Perhaps he just slept in his clothes or maybe there was a hidden tarp in his box or plastic similar to the standard fire fighter's shelter. He was a tough old man.

We passed a dilapidated outhouse which ravens flew through. The spindly spruces lining the banks in monotonous rows looked like matchwood in the moonlight. Skyline and water were exactly the same shade. The ducks and geese on the lakes would wait until freeze-up before they left.

Jupiter was high in the southern sky. Later, when Jupiter was photographed by the space module and shown in color, my instant smug recognition would be that artists have visualized and painted abstractions that resembled it for years.

"I had a waitress work on the boat who said she'd never live in Alaska," said the captain, lighting his pipe. "She came up for a summer to work and saw those scrawny trees along the Yukon and said, 'How could I make a living here if those trees are so spindly and short and have to struggle so hard to grow?' "

The river beat against the six-foot-high banks, eroding them. This flat country was full of lakes and islands; I would be hard put to find the main channel. The low landscape had a monotony except for the pattern of sandy, gravelly banks.

The captain steered the boat to the undercut banks, where the water was deeper. Then he relaxed and reminisced: "When I was twenty-two I went to Nome to seek my fortune. I slept on the beach in a sleeping bag until I got a job running a drill at a mine."

At three-thirty in the eerie morning dark, we arrived at Stevens Village. It had been a restless night. I went out on the slippery decks to see the village and was rewarded by a shadowed moon, a starlit night and a lingering display of northern lights. The villagers were sensibly in their beds; one harsh voice shouted "Shut up!" to a screeching malamute.

Dawn illuminated the early morning, lighting the weather-beaten log houses. I went back to bed and read *I Heard an Owl Call My Name*, by Margaret Craven, a clean, beautiful book about Indians that I wished I could have written. The same legend about the owl's predicting death existed among Athabaskans. I wondered if that young girl freezing alone on the trail had heard an owl.

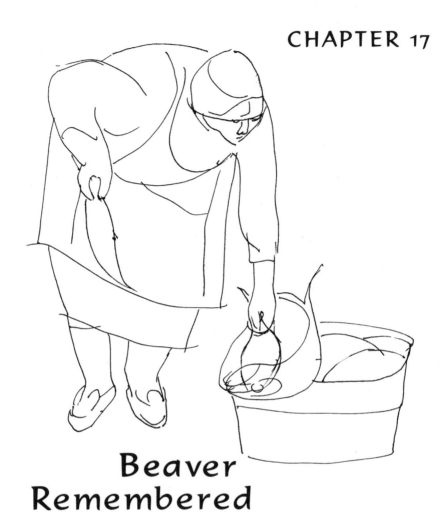

CHAPTER 17

Beaver
Remembered

January: Trapping season.
February: Beaver season. Jigging for pike and whitefish under ice.
March: Days getting longer, hunting rabbits and grouse.
April: Muskrats, mallards, pintails.
May: End of ducks and geese. River ice breakup. Sandhill cranes go over.
June: Fishing begins.
July: King salmon time.
August: Silver and dog salmon fishing.
September: Moose hunting, getting wood.
October: River running ice.
November: The ice is solid. Trapping begins.
December: Christmas.

THE CYCLE AT BEAVER

In Beaver, Indians, Eskimos, Japanese and an occasional white trapper have lived peacefully together. The land originally was used by bands of Yukon Flat Kutchin and Koyukon Indians, who fished and hunted there.

A Japanese by the name of Frank Yasuda and a group of Eskimos established the first little settlement at Beaver. Yasuda, a seaman on the U.S. revenue cutter *Bear,* jumped ship to remain at Barrow, marrying an Eskimo woman named Nevelo. He worked for Charlie Brower's whaling company until the demand for whale oil and whalebone declined. Two prospectors, Marsh and Carter, hired the industrious Yasuda, luring him with promises of gold in the Chandalar area.

In 1904, Frank, Nevelo and two Eskimos left Barrow by dog team to meet Marsh and Carter, arriving after a torturous trip.

Other Eskimos heard of their later gold strike, and fourteen families left their ancestral homes with loaded dog sleds to undertake the long journey to join Yasuda. They took almost two years, crossing the Brooks Range on the way according to Turak, one of the original settlers of Beaver.

During the long trek through the wilderness, there were several deaths and one birth. It was winter in the range, a time of blizzards and below-zero weather. The small party of Eskimo men, women and children traveled by snowy trails through one mountain pass and over another, hunting as they went, living on caribou, mountain sheep and fish.

Heading south, they followed icy rivers, hills and rocky terrain. They were familiar with the northern Arctic coastal area but had never traveled this far inland. They had never been in a forest; they had never seen a moose. When they did taste moose meat, the children cried that it tasted like wood and would not eat it, used as they were to seal and whale meat.

The fur-clad women were capable skin sewers and accustomed to butchering meat. They traveled many miles by dog team each day, sitting on the heavily laden sleds or trudging behind on snowshoes.

One woman conceived on the trail. When it was time to give birth, she was on snowshoes. It was the time of a terrible blizzard; snow raged around the mountains, whipping the flakes to a white fury until the nearest hills were no longer visible. When her cramps began, she doubled over with pain. There was no time to put up the tent; the child was ready to be born. The women related that "she kicked off her snowshoes, lay down on a caribou skin and gave birth right on the ice."

Perhaps they stopped afterward to make tea and make camp; perhaps they did not. No one remembered.

The mother was strong and healthy, for Arctic Indian and Eskimo women alike were used to giving birth in isolation and walking afterward on the trail. Women walked out alone, dropped their babies and walked back with the newborns in their parkas.

One of the children carried on his mother's back on this long trek was not so fortunate, for he froze to death. The family stopped long enough to sew the dead boy into a seal poke.

The small struggling band of Eskimos arrived in the summer of 1913, their belongings on their backs and on the backs of their dogs. Walking the last few miles, following rivers and game trails, they abandoned their sleds, as without snow the sleds were useless on the rocky terrain full of moss and hummocks. There on the Yukon they were reunited with the Yasudas; there they learned for the first time to build log cabins aboveground, white man's style, instead of the underground sod houses of the Arctic; there they changed their diets from seal and whale meat to caribou and moose meat; and there they learned to get along with their neighbors, the Athabaskan Indians.

Yasuda established a freight business and trading post at Beaver, since it was a river terminus for miners heading north to the gold fields. They raised oats and hay in the summer to feed the horses; winters were sixty below zero. Indians came to visit the post to trade, and found Yasuda agreeable, exchanging furs for food.

For forty years Yasuda grubstaked miners and Indians, building a one-room schoolhouse for the children. Charley Mayse, who trapped at Beaver Creek, told me that Yasuda always had credit on the books and never sold liquor. "He was an easygoing man, well liked. A gentle man who didn't like to hunt. He walked to Fairbanks often."

As our boat neared Beaver, I recalled my last stay there six years ago. Charley had arranged for me to stay with Mrs. Charlotte Adams, a widow. Her ten-year-old log house was weather-beaten to a gray patina. I set down my sleeping bag, paint box, rucksack and a box containing meat, eggs and fresh vegetables for her and Charley.

The widow's soft olive complexion and deep-set melancholy black eyes revealed a depth of compassion and suffering. She stood straight and smiled warmly, pointing to one of the beds: "That's yours." I protested that I had brought my own sleeping bag; I knew her sheets

Charlotte

had to be washed with river water, packed laboriously uphill in five-gallon cans, but she would not hear of my sleeping in a bag.

Charlotte, or "Grandma," as everyone called her, was raised in Chalkyitsik on the Black River. Her father, Frank Foster, was a trapper, and her mother a Fort Yukon Indian; her grandparents raised her. Her family, working their way down the Yukon, decided to settle at Beaver.

Brown-gray hair tied loosely fell over Charlotte's sloping shoulders. She walked like a young girl, with a soft, gliding grace, possessing a delicacy in spite of her age. After her first husband died, she married Salvan Adams, of Koyukuk, who died of tuberculosis. Her house was the center of the village and her kerosene lantern burned steadily all night.

Among the log houses, outhouses, caches, drying racks, smoke-houses and dog houses was the trading post. A few feet away flowed the Yukon, with its compelling rush of sucking river. The sun glistened on the wide sand bars and twisting labyrinthine passages; the water was opaque with pulverized rock and glacial powder. During spring breakup, the ice-jammed banks caved in, and trees plummeted into the river, sometimes causing it to rise.

Jack Van Hatten, a trader who had settled in Beaver in the early fifties, had the satisfied look of a man being exactly where he wanted to be and doing exactly what he wanted to do. A short, rotund man in his seventies, he said, "Ivar Peterson used to own this post and he sold it to me. Ivar used to say, 'Why people broke? Woods full of money!' "

Jack said that nearly every family had a check from welfare. "They buy booze from Rampart. I won't sell it. Can't stand to see the malnutrition and TB come in when they spend the money on booze.

"My wife died when the kids were five years old, so I had to work hard to take care of them. I flew a plane in those days, no instruments. Picked up furs, traded, trapped—it wasn't easy. I like to live close to nature. Used to be only twenty-seven families here. The old people died. Now there are only seventy-five people.

"No one works except at fire fighting. No way to make money here. We just trade work for moose meat. The women don't marry— they get checks for each child they support. Some have five or six from different men and they play the field. They want it that way; if they married, their checks would stop. They make more that way. Husbands are unnecessary. Women here shoot and hunt and fish as well as a man."

Charlotte's house had three stoves. One was a big wood stove for winter months when the temperature dropped to sixty below zero, one a barrel stove and the other a small airtight stove used for quick meals in the summer. "It lasts one year. Too thin," said Charlotte. "You fill it with paper, wood and one match, and away it goes. Bam! Tea in one minute."

Charlotte's grandchildren loved to stay with her, for she was patient and gentle, rarely raising her voice in anger. Often sighing with deep resignation, she would say, arms folded over her stomach, "Poor so-and-so," with compassion. I never heard her say an unkind word about anyone. The women trusted her to deliver their babies.

During the day Charlotte cut fish for her drying rack. Ulak, an Eskimo neighbor, carried her salmon halter fashion, in two wooden buckets slung over his shoulders. Dog salmon was packed into the buckets, tails and heads flopping as Ulak carried them uphill, dumping them on cardboard spread out on the grass.

Charlotte stood at an old wood table, clad in an apron over her black dress, her hair pulled back in a net. Whetting the knife on a black stone, she slit the fish right up one side as casually and easily as I butter bread. Out plopped the liver, spleen and entrails. She slit the backbone, scaled and slivered the salmon. The parts she kept for the dogs went into one washtub; the slit fish slid into another. Later she hung it on the pole rack to dry.

All was done without a single wasted motion. Blood spilled deep into the wood table, not spattering her white apron; except for bloody hands she remained clean, a skill handed down through generations of Indian river women. The cleaning of fish was considered a religious act.

"A long time ago we had nets and fishwheels all up and down the river. All the women and girls cut fish. I'm the only one here now," said Charlotte, sharpening her knife carefully. "I'm doing this mostly for my son and his wife to feed their dogs."

The best salmon she cut more carefully, with closer slits to dry faster. It was called "squaw candy" by whites. One huge pike half her size went into the pile for the dogs. "One thing we never buy, that's fish and moose meat," Charlotte said, proudly slapping another dog salmon on the table. "If we had a cold freezer we could freeze fish."

In southeastern Alaska the delicacy is salmon fish heads. I ate fish eyes at a Tlingit Indian potlatch once but can't say I relished them. Children chew fish air sacs like bubble gum. They taste terrible, bitter like metal. Heart and liver are delicious, except for the spleen.

I tried to help Charlotte cut fish, but it was at the risk of losing a finger, so I decided to stick to my drawing.

I painted Charlotte as she cut fish, blowflies surrounding us and the pile of salmon growing on the racks.

In the evening a huge orange moon hung over the Yukon. In the cabin, with Charley visiting, we talked by kerosene light. "This is the way we made our blankets out of rabbit skin," Charlotte said, showing me how she cut the rabbit in one-inch widths, rolled it on a piece of wood, then knotted it loosely, like a fisherman's net. The whole blanket could then be folded up in a small space when camping. "Fur is warmer and lighter. It traps the air that way," she said.

"They're warm all right, but you wind up with lots of rabbit fur in your mouth, nose and eyes," Charley added.

Charlotte sipped her tea. "I thought nothing of going camping. The weather never made any difference, no matter what the temperature. Nowadays the boys won't go when it's cold. 'Too cold,' they say. They don't have the right clothes. We used to have long caribou clothing, fur mitts, warm blanket and moccasins. Sleep in tents. When a boy of twelve from Fairbanks came to stay with me, he didn't even know how to cut wood. Why, he couldn't even pack water.

"Beaver seems dead now, not like it used to be, full of busy people, store packed with all manner of goods. Steamboats used to come down the Yukon past Beaver. They had to have lots of wood for fuel, and hired men to cut wood at five dollars a cord. Men used to have camps every five miles along the river."

Jack came over to "borrow" some of the dried moose meat hanging over her stove.

"He," says Charlotte, meaning one of the women, "has no husband but lots of kids." Charlotte and the other village women and men say "he" for "she" and "she" for "he."

"They have no dances here," said Jack, chewing the moose meat with relish. "No Indian dances like Minto or Fort Yukon, and no Eskimo dances like Barrow. The missionaries stopped it years ago." When the two cultures, Indian and Eskimo, met and could not understand each other, they learned English. But the missionaries almost eliminated both cultures.

The schoolteacher and his son shot two moose. There was much speculation around the village that the two teachers would not need all that meat for just the two of them, since their sons would leave soon for college. Everyone knew everyone's business, hours, even minutes, after it happened.

Charley Mayse had been busy getting his gear together for the trapping season. Charley had come to Beaver in 1949, trapping and canoeing the wilderness riverways. His small cabin was crowded with twenty years of paraphernalia: all manner of chipped mugs, pots, rifles, special tools and equipment such as his life style required. Old magazines and books were piled up precariously everywhere, and on his bed were the supplies that he was planning to take with him to the trap line. He cleared the table with the side of his hand.

"When I first came to Beaver, the Indians were not drinking. They lived closer to the land," he said. He froze in one year at his Beaver River trapping camp and had to wait there one month before he could get out. "I was merely drifting downstream early in October when Birch Stream froze up, leaving me stranded. I was making a little scouting trip, had a tent as usual and camping equipment.

"I was missing thirty days, but I wasn't lost. People were wondering what happened to me. I had some grub, enough for two weeks. I made it last a month. Using snares, I soon exhausted the rabbit population. When they found me I still had a rabbit and two prunes." I recalled how worried we were in Fairbanks, but Charlie could not understand why all the fuss was being made.

Indians rarely trap alone like white men. They prefer to share trail life. They live in the wilderness most of the time and do not need to get away to be alone like white men do.

Charley was sorting out his stuff. "Takes lots of thinking. I need three axes, one for each cabin." If he forgot something he could not come back for it and had to do without it; on the other hand, he did not want to pack too much.

"The name Beaver," said Turak the Eskimo, crossing his legs, "was probably because a miner saw a beaver crossing the river and so the name stuck."

Turak had worked in the gold mines, freighted and trapped and was a good carpenter. When he was fifteen he had followed Yasuda. "We came down from Barrow over the Brooks Range by dog team, shooting game all the way.

"We loaded the dogs down with packs filled with meat. I climbed up to the summit with about eighty pounds on my back. There was fog right down to the ground. We kept winding through a kind of valley. I measured the snow with my walking stick and it was four feet deep, but we didn't sink down more than two inches because it was hard-packed. Six miles later everything was green and lots of mosquitoes. We built a log raft and some of us went on the raft. We didn't have anything to eat, only Allashuk's wife—she generally saved a little bit for the children, a little dry meat and a little fat . . .

"Olla went ahead to try to get a moose or caribou. We were sitting on the raft and the current was slow. On a little slough, there was Olla holding up a big moose ham. When we landed there and walked up, he had fat ribs roasting on a campfire. He was expecting us to come by. Hungry, oh boy, we filled up on that fat meat! We were all right for another week. That is the last game we got. We ran out of flour and tea."

Turak now received a pension check and in addition ran a little store in his one-room cabin, selling candy, hardtack, flour and sugar.

Ducks flew over the village and squirrels ran along the caches and the fish racks, trying to steal food. Birds twittered, wings fluttered, flies buzzed and the fishwheel squeaked. Occasionally the children spoke as they drew with crayons, breaking the silence.

Ulak emptied the nets of forty fish, and Charlotte and a friend cut fish all day. A smudge fire burned in the shed and the oil dripped slowly off the sliced fish.

I felt clumsy watching their deftness, and to pacify my guilt I gave the children art lessons and treated them all to candy bars, knowing full well that would help rot their teeth.

Every day Charlotte stood in her white apron and black dress, cutting orange salmon under a blue sky.

Her compassion for all things human and animal was revealed in her love for little insects and birds. She would not kill little bugs or birds who stole from her fish rack. She berated a woman who once killed a squirrel because he ate from her fish rack. "The little he ate! He's got to live too," she said, then added softly, "Squirrels good to eat roasted over a hot fire. We eat muskrats, beaver, everything."

Her movements were gentle and dignified. I loved her. She sometimes called me "Ba-by." I gave a drawing of her granddaughter Bonnie to her. One of her daughters, Minnie, who was blind, lived in Fairbanks, and the youngest daughter, Anne, married Scott Fischer, an Episcopal priest.

Charlotte dug out of her cold cellar the two chickens I had brought and invited Jack, Ulak and the grandchildren to a feast. The Sunday menu read:

> Curried chicken à la Charlotte
> Rutabagas . . . potatoes
> Sailor Boy pilot bread and butter
> Strong tea

Charlotte's ten-year-old black dog lay tied up, docile and arthritic, behind the house. Once a year he was brought out and harnessed for the children's dog race, and the old champion still won, his only glory in old age.

The gentle dog did not bark at me as I passed him on the way to the outhouse. The red-orange moon was my candle, pouring into the darkness. A mouse crept under the wooden door, startling me.

At evening we turned on the radio program *Tundra Topics*. Charlotte listened religiously to the announcements: "Margaret Charlie wants her mother to send her salmon strips," "Reverend Luke Titus will be arriving the airport Wednesday at Fort Yukon," and so on.

We sat around the stove talking about trapping. "It's a way of life I like," Charley said, crossing his leg. "I don't have to think."

"My grandfather just took some tea, ax and salt," said Charlotte as she put another log into the fire. "Took off with team, never planned or think about it. Just go. Stayed two weeks, trapped, shot grouse, everything. Just threw in sled."

Charlotte loved "to hunt alone, kill moose, skin it. Build fire, lay down in my clothes with my arm over my head, no blanket. Spend the night laying down in the woods on spruce bed." Even the elderly school cook had a snare line and a fish trap.

Once when Charlotte went down to the lake to check her traps, she heard wolves howling. When she walked back to the camp she saw tracks in her trail but thought it was her dog following. Arriving back at camp, she saw that her dog was tied up. "It must have been a wolf following me," she said.

"In the winter the kids go after school to trap and hunt with a lard can and candle in it," said Charlotte. "It's too cold for flashlight batteries. They shoot lynx, rabbits. Sometimes they get mink, fox and marten in their snares and traps." They walked in the dark snowy evenings with a bit of bread or pilot bread in their pockets.

Charlotte remembered the first animal that her son Cliff had killed. He was three when she put him on her lap to aim the rifle at a tree squirrel. He shot his first moose at twelve.

At nine in the morning Ulak came to take us across the river to get fish from Charlotte's net. He waited while I hurriedly dressed and had a quick cup of coffee. It was a gray day with little sun, and I was glad because my face was burnt red on one side from painting in the sun.

Ulak took Charlotte and me across the Yukon in a motorboat, pointing out the Winers' fish rack. We faced strong winds into Beaver Creek, then into Fish Creek, with the Haystack Mountains in the far distance. The river, about one mile wide, had yellow banks with dark spires of spruce. Geese flew up from the banks. "Honkers," grinned Ulak.

Some fish were tangled in the net, alive and wiggling, until Ulak whacked them with his ax handle, then patiently loosened them from the net with his fingers. Soon the bottom of the boat was full of silvers, dog salmon and large silver whitefish with iridescent scales.

We stopped at an old Indian camping ground where fish racks had caved in. Underneath the bank was a cold storage place for fish and berries.

After being out on the river all afternoon, we felt good to climb the banks and come into Charlotte's warm house.

The schoolteachers had cut up their two moose and distributed huge steaks to everyone in the village. The steaks were delicious with the new potatoes Turak gave Charlotte.

All the cabins seemed to have bunches of dried weeds stuck into cans, an attempt by the women to pretty things up. Unique in Charlotte's house was a room divider, made by her granddaughter Bonnie, of Coke can flip tops all hooked into one another. Reverend Tredwell counted a row and said, "Bonnie, do you realize you have one hundred thirty-four dollars hanging there at thirty-five cents a can of pop?"

Charlotte had made the patchwork quilt on the foot of my bed and filled it with goose and duck feathers. Bonnie's cornucopias filled with paper flowers hung on the wall over the kitchen table, along with faded snapshots of Charlotte's twenty-three grandchildren and one souvenir plate.

Ulak asked if I wanted to go rabbit hunting with him, a few miles' walk, but I had promised the children an art lesson. Even the youngest child walked five or six miles after school to hunt and thought nothing of it. The women walked beautifully here, in harmony with the land.

Ulak came back with four rabbits shot only one-half mile away. His house, which used to be Yasuda's old cabin, had burned down last winter, so he lived in his brother's small house, overcrowded with his five children. "Poor Ulak," sighed Charlotte.

One of Ulak's sons strutted and spat like his dad. He had cut the weeds in front of the store for Jack and was spending some of his money on Cokes. Later I saw him lift two heavy pails full of fish with his thin arms. Another son, a fifteen-year-old owlish in his big glasses, helped Grandma with chores. He had stunned a grouse with a rock, then, twisting its neck, carried it into his cabin for the pot. Ulak and his boys toted, hauled, chopped, stowed, packed or carried anything in exchange for grub.

"They named that point after me," Ulak said, pointing upriver. "I had a nice cabin and fishwheel there when my wife was alive."

Fish and moose were Charlotte's mainstay. She stripped some moose fat and hung it to dry at the back of the stove. We ate boiled silver salmon with rice, canned corn, bread and coffee. She made fish soup, like the proverbial chicken soup, to give to sick people.

This was Charlotte's recipe for beaver:

Take off fur, cut head, feet and tail.
Take inside out, take everything out, throw it to the dogs.
Roast in pan with water, onions, if you have them,
    and salt and pepper till done.
Boil tail, cool and slice for sandwiches.
Use beaver fur trim on moccasins.

Down by the river later with Charlotte, I watched children parade with a muskrat on a rope until one boy untied him and he quickly swam away. A boy walked by with fifteen mallards, giving one to Charlotte.

Jay Eisenhardt, about thirty-four and a former Cornell student, had come to Beaver to write his wildlife thesis. He never finished it or went back to Cornell. We met near Charlotte's house. "I've heard of your paintings," he said. I was surprised at that. He trapped, fished and hunted like the old Indians used to do, claiming he didn't want a wife, but Charlotte thought differently. "Which girl wants to live old Indian style anymore! The girls here want to get away; they want washing machines!"

Jay came to Beaver from his camp fifty miles away four times a year for supplies and once at Christmas. In addition to his main cabin, he had nine small trap-line cabins and a fish camp with nine hundred dogfish drying on poles. His garden was full of lettuce, radishes, potatoes and carrots. In the winter he wore a parka that he made of Hudson Bay cloth and fur he trapped. Charlotte showed him how to make a rabbit-skin blanket in the old style from rabbits he snared.

"You should see him come down the Yukon," boasted Charlotte. "Ten dogs sitting in front of him in the boat he built himself."

He had stopped to ask her some particulars about the making of fish strips. When he left, she said wistfully, "He lives more Indian than our own boys do."

A visiting Arctic Village woman sat on the earth chopping and slicing salmon in a spotless white wool kerchief covering her hair. Brushing blowflies off her black dress with the back of her bloody fingers, her hands were seemingly independent of the rest of her.

Her pregnant daughter leaned on the cabin doorway watching her mother cut fish. Indian women used to squat sensibly when labor began. Lying on one's back may be convenient for the modern doctor, but it is not natural for the mother and baby. Why not let gravity help? The Indian woman would squat, alone, cutting the umbilical cord with her thumbnail, then tying it with caribou thongs.

The Arctic Village woman's daughter would probably have a spinal at the Tanana Hospital. "That's if I get there in time," she said, leaning her arm on the doorjamb, the curve of her stomach protruding. If not, there was always Charlotte or her mother to assist.

People seemed lethargic, moving slowly, as in an old movie reel. I was the laziest one of all. Turak said I caught the "Beaver sickness."

Propping up a canvas on a rock, I sat on the Yukon banks tranquilly listening to leaves rustle, watching their reflection in the water, noticing the small ants tumble. The sun shone on an endless mosaic of dark land, hazy gold trees and shimmering water. Cabin smoke streaked the blue sky.

The water looked muddy, but the villagers drank it and so far I was not sick. It reminded me of our water in Fairbanks thirty-three years ago, which turned coffee gray, whiskey black and white diapers orange from the minerals.

I liked walking freely on the trails and through tall grasses; my body enjoyed the freedom. When I was not painting, I stopped to visit in the cabins. Indians used few words, but they were descriptive and to the point. They usually said what they meant or they were silent.

Hardly a boat passed downriver this time of year. "A few people came by motorboat, but they didn't stop," said Jack, the village monarch, who watched everything on the Yukon. "Once I lost ten thousand dollars' worth of grub and furs when my barge overturned. Beaver River is full of rapids further down. If you follow the main channel, you can stay on Yukon pretty good."

Sun beat on his bald spot as he fondled his cat. "Only cat in the village. I killed off all the males. Didn't want cats all over the place."

I visited Monkman's cabin at the end of the road. He was not the average Beaver Indian; turquoise rings and a large wristwatch covered his white arms. No one seemed to know where he came from. The children were frightened of him and said he talked to himself and shot his rifle into the air.

"He has no wife, nothing," said Charlotte.

Jack and Monkman said that Fairbanks air smelled of dirty oil— Fairbanks, the town I love. But comparing it with Beaver, they are right. Except for two trucks, there is no machinery in Beaver.

Cardboard milk cartons were nailed over Monkman's wall to insulate his small cabin. Two neat cots, a small primus stove, some clothes and his gun filled the dark interior. His garden was full of spuds, cabbages and carrots, and a porch stored his wood and tools.

"I like a small cabin, easy to heat and care for," Monkman said. Pushing his hat so that the feather perched over his nose and digging into an old suitcase, he brought out photos of himself in full Sioux dance costume.

"I was born on the Yukon, but I lived on a Sioux reservation for eight years. I fell and hurt my back during the earthquake. Can't work hard anymore."

Monkman looked at my drawing of Bonnie and asked what I would charge to paint someone in Indian costume.

I had watched him dance at a Fairbanks potlatch in full Sioux regalia, including a long feather headdress, the kind one rarely sees up north. He marched in the Fairbanks parades, a solitary Indian behind a float symbolizing pioneer days, ceremoniously putting one foot straight ahead of the other.

Dawn broke in splashes of yellow over the dwellings, lightening the sleeping dogs curled in the grasses. Gnat bites on my ankles and drops of rain splattering on the tin roof kept me awake throughout the night. The end of September brought continued sunshine and white flowers. Dog fennel grew wild everyplace.

The tundra in autumn was a speckled pattern of yellow-orange land and rusty birch, the earth a faded green of dried-up riverbeds. New snow had fallen on the mountains and a huge rainbow hovered over it. Rainbows always signified good fortune for me, since I was born on such a day.

I painted by the river and in the woods, the sun beating on my orange sweater, making me part of the landscape. Black ravens dipped and hawked at me and the river as a flat-bottomed boat thumped by.

The children played along beside me like little puppies in the foxtails. "Look, Clara, I can do a tumble," cried one. They painted with my watercolors.

The bloody, butchered moose head and two dead rabbits lay on the Winers' floor, bounty from their hunting trip. The Winers had fifteen dogs to feed in addition to seven blind, wiggly pups. Their large family included an eight-month-old baby and a mongoloid with a bad heart, who lay suffering in the middle of an old mattress.

The Winers were related to the original Eskimo families who had come down from Barrow. It was Mrs. Winer's mother who had given birth on the trail during the blizzard. The children posed with natural grace. "Draw me, draw me," they implored, their tousled heads near their puppies. Too bad I was not a calendar artist.

In his relaxed way George Winer was a very resourceful man, capable of adapting to every emergency, especially adept at fixing machinery, hunting and fishing. His ragged, barefoot children played imaginative games with scraps of blankets, old beds, pups, sticks of wood, anything, each busy living every minute in the sun.

I awoke one morning to hear the sound of Alfred Pitka's saw cutting wood for Charlotte. He also carried water for her, and for this he received a bit of meat or fish, sometimes a dollar or more. I was alone in the house when he came in and sat quietly, looking grotesque, gnarled and silent as a piece of wood. When I grabbed my sketch pad and went out the back door to visit Shirley Tredwell, the minister's wife, he followed me.

Shirley said, "He's harmless. He will just sit quietly until you tell him to go." I painted his sad face full of lumps and wrinkles; it reminded me of one of the men in Van Gogh's "Potato Eaters." Although his hands were deformed, he managed them usefully, hauling and chopping. He had a place in the village, everyone knew him; he was not just shunted into a corner and hidden as sometimes happens in our society with brain-damaged people.

The season switched from salmon fishing to moose hunting, and four moose were shot. Ulak drank coffee with fingers swollen and infected from fish and slime getting into his cuts. "Can't find a band-aid. Not any in the store or anyplace!" he said as he prepared to go moose hunting.

Blind David Adams, Charlotte's brother-in-law from Stevens Village, joined us, and I poured him a cup of coffee. He was deaf, too, so I had to yell into his ear. His wife had died since I had seen him last.

David had a dark, intense face with a ragged haircut. His shoulders hunched aggressively in his red jacket and faded blue workshirt. His voice grunted short answers as his gnarled hands smoothed his cane.

He liked to visit his children in different villages. He chopped his own wood and was known to travel twenty-five miles by himself in temperatures of sixty below zero. The island above Stevens was named after him. "People say that's my island. I used to fish there," said David, leaning on his willow cane. "There used to be so many people traveling on the river that canoes stretched for two bends in the slough."

I bequeathed my extra watercolor set to Bonnie, Charlotte's granddaughter, who had been my best pupil. Charlotte had packed two king salmon for me. The children were dressed for school. Gone were the weeds in their tumbled hair; gone were the bare, dirty feet. They marched like proper schoolchildren in new shoes to the ring of the school bell. Charlotte and I watched fondly as they trouped past our doorway and waved good-by.

CHAPTER 18

Beaver Revisited

The snow geese and the ducks are coming in
At the mouth of the Yukon.
You can see the orange color of the sky at dawn.

DANIEL JOHN,
"Song of the Snow Geese."
Recorded by Thomas F. Johnston

MY previous trip to Beaver had been a memorable one due mainly to Charlotte Adams, a loving spirit. Now as I stood on the decks of *The Tanana,* I scanned the figures silhouetted against the flaming sky, looking eagerly for her. In the six years that intervened, I had seen Charlotte a few times in Fairbanks. Charley Mayse, Charlotte and I had enjoyed a reunion dinner at my home on one of her trips to Fairbanks.

The children at Beaver were bunched in dark forms, hopping up and down at the sight of our boat. The Winer family was out watching the unloading, the children clinging to the parents' sides. There was a new pair of twins; the sickly baby had died.

I ran into Charlotte on the way to her home. It was dark and she was not expecting me, had no idea I was on the boat. We hugged and kissed each other in a grand reunion, and holding hands to avoid the potholes, we walked back to her cabin.

Her cabin was lovely in the glow of her kerosene lamp, the table covered in red-checkered cloth, laid as if for guests. I put down the candy and fruit I had brought as she bustled about making tea. Her dear face had new lines and her feet were clothed in the familiar black cotton stockings. She was the same gentle soul in her wonderful simplicity and love, still mixing her "she's" and "he's," her voice as soft as ever. Things had changed; women were now fire fighting. Charlotte had thirty-two grandchildren and her son had "split the blanket" with his wife.

I had just missed Jay Eisenhardt, who had come to Beaver on one of his infrequent visits.

"No radio even," said Charlotte.

"Does he have a wife yet?" I asked.

"No," she answered.

"All our young people have left for school," said Charlotte sadly later. "It's lonely in the village without them."

She told me how Ulak had died. "You know the little pool of water? She [meaning he] went in to play with the children. She went down once, laughing, twice, but the third time didn't come up. Drown. They bring Ulak up, but it was too late."

"Was it deep?"

"No. It was heart attack. Afterwards they found all kinds of pills under the bed for blood pressure. Doctor gave it, but Ulak never take it. I miss my friend so. Poor man. His son goes to New Mexico to school."

Alfred came in and stood awkwardly, his head hung low.

"Poor thing," said Charlotte.

"He works hard chopping wood and hauling water. Why call him 'poor thing'?" I asked.

"His mind is not good."

I introduced Charlotte to Captain Brown and asked if I could show her the boat, as in all these years she never had been on it. The captain gave permission and we walked over the wet plank and the cables to my room to show her my paintings; then up to the wheelhouse and down to the messhall. Afterward we stood on the deck watching a large display of moving northern lights, red and green curtains, spectacular lights flashing over the village. We parted reluctantly; the boat was leaving the next morning.

Jack Van Hatten had sold his store to the village council, which had been given a hundred-thousand-dollar loan from the Native corporation. The council had appointed a new manager; the people would be responsible for their own food supply now. Jack had had much power in the village, since it had been up to him to extend or cut off credit. The people resented the situation now, and Jack felt their hostility.

"The revolution is coming," he said. "They will find out that my prices were not so high when they buy food wholesale and add the high cost of freight. People don't pay bills. I used to wait by the post office to collect when they got their relief checks. The town is going down. People still owe me money, but I guess I'll never get it."

Beaver needed to find an industry to make the village self-supporting. The men were restless. Hunting was their love and their blood. It was too bad that hunting could not be made an industry, for it lent interest, substance and excitement to their lives. When there was not enough game and the government relief checks supplied food, they lost all incentive.

I asked Jack how the village voted in the last election.

"No one voted, not even me."

"What about the Hensley and Hickel signs posted?"

"Oh, the politicians fly down, stop for a minute, put up a sign and then leave."

"What about Stevens Village?"

"Probably the same. I used to get ballots and have voting places, but it's too much trouble." He shrugged his shoulders. The village is so out of touch with the world. The river goes by, but news rarely reaches this remote village.

We watched boys unloading new cartons of foodstuffs for the co-op on the riverbanks. "Someone better come and get them or the bears will," mumbled Jack.

With the emergence of Indian power, young people were beginning to shoulder more responsibility, yet they also showed more hostility. Charley Mayse was angry that his water barrel had been knocked over and rocks thrown through his cabin windows.

We pulled out of Beaver in the morning. Willows, cottonwoods and aspens were a varicolored green, yellow and orange mosaic, the ground cover a dulled red. The forest smelled pungent and sweet with its mixture of rotted mushrooms and berries. The river was full of islands, the large ones bearing large spruce. The captain's map showed places named Natine, Kutcha, Athapaska . . . No one lived in them now.

Back on the boat the men ate in silence. One had to shout to be heard over the motors. I tried to make conversation, but it was hard, as no one volunteered a word. The Indian deck hands who ate in the other room usually stuck to meat and turned down salad and sweets. They too were silent.

The boat veered through the Yukon Flats' intricate channels. The river sprawled through and spilled into myriad channels, inlets, bogs and swamps.

The first white man who ever voyaged through the Flats and upper Yukon was Alexander H. Murray. "I must say that as I sat smoking my pipe," he wrote, "my face besmeared with tobacco juice to keep at bay the mosquitoes still hovering in clouds around me, my first impressions of the Yukon were anything but favorable. I never saw an uglier river, everywhere low banks, with lakes and swamps, the trees too small for building, the water abominably dirty, and the current furious."

A map of the Yukon Flats showed the river to twist and turn like a demented thing. The flats were like a gigantic curved basin full of migratory birds, mosquito breeding grounds and boggy ponds— thirty-six thousand of them, by one estimate. Over two million ducks, geese and swans were born here each year. On the edges grew wild celery, cowslip, sour dock and goose grass.

From May to September the air was alive with cries and wing beats of migrating birds. Emperor, Canada and snow geese nested there, as did thousands of baldpates, pintails, golden eye and old squaw ducks, sandhill cranes and pure white trumpeter swans, eiders, loons and species of shore birds, all filling the air with their raucous music. The Arctic tern came from Argentina, the golden plover from the Galápagos Islands and the small wheatear flew five thousand miles from Africa to nest in the surrounding hills.

The Army Corps of Engineers, backed by Senator Gruening when he was alive, wanted to build Rampart Dam to create electric power to change the flats into one gigantic inland lake. The Indians hated the proposal even though it meant temporary jobs. One Indian reacted in a typical way: "What are we supposed to do, drown or something?" It would have ended their life style and hunting habits and taken away the nesting grounds of migratory birds and animal life.

The dammed-up Yukon would have meant the death of a great river, the end of the salmon runs and a disaster for the Indians. The Yukon is and must ever be a free-flowing, living force. Environmentalists fought the construction of the dam and won; the project had little congressional support. The flats remain, in all their bizarre splendor.

CHAPTER 19

Fort Yukon

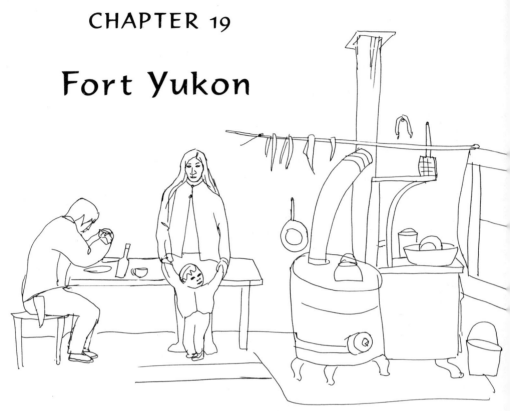

Han ji' ti'i haa ihkwaa   I canoe upriver
    Ł'haa chuu nint'aii   Against the stream
    lhtree k'it t'ihchy'aa   The water is very swift
    lhdlaa k'it t'ihchy'aa   Just like I'm crying
    Oonjit nijin gwats'a'   Just like I'm laughing

       T'ishi'in gwaał'in   I know where I'm going
       Chihkhal googaa   And I can see the place
    Nihk'it hekłan ihkwaa   But no matter how hard I paddle
                       I am still at the same place

KATHERINE PETER, *Gineerinylyaa*

G<small>EESE</small> were honking over the boat, flying in two large formations, with stragglers trying to catch up. Wind rippled on the sand bars, and logs jutted out into the main stream of the river. Short fringes of trees lined the banks, and beyond them was nothing but vast skies as on the prairies, skies pale at the perimeter.

The Fort Yukon Indians of the Kutchin tribe used to live in dome-shaped dwellings of curved willows covered with caribou skins. Twenty-five years ago, when I visited Fort Yukon, there was a trading post, some helter-skelter cabins and dirt trails between them. Now Fort Yukon is the largest village on the Yukon, with a population of about seven hundred people.

As our boat neared, I could see mud swallows nesting in the riverbanks and some old deserted shacks covered with flattened Standard Oil cans. A few fishwheels sagged against the flats. Where banks of berries shone, lone small red leaves still clung to withered bushes.

The ship's throaty whistle was loud, piercing the stillness, and out of nowhere people came running, dogs barking at their heels. Wide gravel streets now held trucks and motorbikes throwing dust.

Captain Brown offered to show me the town, stopping first at the Northern Commercial store. The young manager, Grafton, remembered me. "I used to see you get off the plane at Kotzebue with your paint box. I used to work for Wien Airlines."

The store was the only one in town; another co-op grocery was being built with a loan from the Native corporation. The price of food was incredibly high because of freight costs. Getting a moose was a necessity; there was no butcher store. When the caribou ran, every man in town left whatever he was doing and headed for the hillsides. At Galena someone called out, "The fish are running," and twenty Indian construction workers deserted the job, leaving wet cement.

An old-timer in the store told me that he used to go fifty miles with his dog team to trade in the early days. "It took me six days to come to Fort Yukon. I traded my furs to buy sugar, salt, flour and ammunition. The best furs and beadwork on the river used to be traded right here. Thousands of marten, otter, beaver and fox pelts used to hang in the store.

"I used to cut one cord of wood in one and a half hours with a straight saw," he said as he shook his head, watching the new forklift handle the cases of milk cartons.

Captain Brown dropped me off at the Sourdough Hotel, since Fort Yukon was the last stop before the boat turned back. I wanted to stay on, and rented a front room facing the river. The hotel, originally at Eagle, 150 miles to the southeast, was dismantled, brought to Circle and finally freighted to Fort Yukon by barge. The ceiling of my room was about nine feet high. Green oilcloth with exposed electrical wiring crawling all over it covered the walls. Bathroom and showers were down the hall. In spite of new curtains and a rug on the floor, the hotel with its uneven floors made me feel uneasy.

June, the attractive young owner, had her work cut out for her as chief cook and bottle washer, front-desk clerk, plumber and whatever else it took to keep the hotel running. June felt she was not fully accepted because she was an Indian from another village. She slapped down a juicy hamburger and fries in front of a young man who joined me in the dining room.

"The Indians here don't want to get ahead," he said. "They'll work a short while, then spend everything on a boat or a Sno-go. They don't care about next month or next year. They just work for now. I look ahead to the future and try to put away for a rainy day. Then they resent what I have, say I got rich on them, because I've got a nicer home. If they want to borrow money from me, I say I can't lend it. Then they call me 'white man.' "

Father Jetté had understood this problem very well when he wrote: "If an Indian deals with a white man, he will expect as much and more than he would from his fellows because a white man has more . . . When the white man is reduced to absolute poverty, living from hand to mouth, then the Indians treat him as an equal, as one of their own."

An Indian at another table explained how he felt: "We have a hard time. No money. On the other hand, why should we work when we get that money coming in? Our father and mother had no money; they don't think about money; they worked with the ax, with tools. Some Indians can live with white people, but many can't live the white people's life. We don't have the education, never went to high school. Some of us go to school and then when we go back into the village, we can't live in the village, either. We go back and forth, trapped between two cultures."

A young man who had quit college after two years said, "Our people are laborers. In the villages we don't see native teachers or lawyers." Some of his young friends were dying, killing themselves with alcohol, some committing suicide. There were incredible pressures on their identities, and drugs were not uncommon. Social life consisted mainly of visiting each other and watching TV, which came on at noon.

The Eskimo guide here on a hunting trip slept in the hotel room next to mine, and I was grateful he did not smoke. The last thing Captain Brown said to me as he dumped my bag off was "In case of fire, jump out the window."

The Sourdough Hotel held memories of prospectors searching for gold, white hunters, fur traders, politicians and whores. What stories the old walls could tell! When I opened the window in the morning, the entire section of glass pane fell out on the little porch. Intact.

The porch sloped dangerously on the second story and I was afraid to venture out to its end. Grease from the frying hamburgers wafted up. A movie house called the Purple Onion was located right next to the hotel. A motley pair.

The Eskimo guide was leaving to climb the Brooks Range to hunt sheep. His client, a burly farmer now in the construction business, was here for his third hunt, "to even up the score with a grizzly who chewed up my rifle last time. No use going out of camp to hunt. He'll find us. Last year they smelled our bacon and there were grizzlies all over the place," boasted the ex-chicken farmer.

Nancy James, the mayor of Fort Yukon, was a determined young woman of twenty-five. "There is another woman mayor in Galena and one in Ruby," she said, adjusting her dark glasses.

We spoke of Dee Olin, the beautiful young mayor of Ruby, known as a capable and hard-working woman dedicated to her people. Indian women seemed to be making progress as leaders and were aggressive speakers against injustice. Perhaps their old matriarchal roles in village life made them natural leaders. The men were often on the go, on the hunt or off to another place for jobs, and could not always be present in office.

Nancy shifted her weight on one foot and looked me directly in the eye. "I'd like to accomplish something for this town."

"What are the problems?"

"The biggest one is alcoholism," answered Nancy, emphasizing her speech with a strong arm movement. "The biggest shock Indians suffered was the culture shock of whites coming in, bringing alcohol and running everything, like the Bureau of Indian Affairs. Some of the missionaries did a lot of good. But Fort Yukon Indians began doing whatever the white people told them to do: 'Go on relief, do this and do that.' Pretty soon they had no voice at all. The town didn't belong to them. But young Indians are beginning to wake up now and speak out."

"How did you get into politics?" I asked.

"I was always interested in politics. I went to meetings. I ran for mayor and got elected. Now I travel everywhere. I am in Doyon, rural C.A.P. [Community Action Program] and other organizations. I go to New York, Fairbanks, Barrow, all over Alaska, and meet many people."

"Would you say you have had a hard life?" I asked.

"It was hard, but it was good. I was brought up in fish camp out of town in summer and on trap line in winter. My dad is a trapper and a pilot on a barge going to Circle. Mom is at fish camp. We always had to work hard."

Nancy, rooted in Indian culture, felt "education was the main thing," so she took correspondence courses in education from the University of Alaska. (Fifty-four percent of Native students drop out of high school and 10 percent out of college.) I told her how I began to paint through the free WPA art classes, and offered to give art lessons to the Fort Yukon children.

The spruces stood tall and eerie in the moonlight and wind. Saturday night in Fort Yukon was quiet except for the whimpering and yowling of the huskies straining at their chains.

"No bars at Fort Yukon. This is a dry town. People voted to have it dry," June said, mopping up the floor. "That doesn't stop them from buying liquor and drinking it at home or at parties."

One resident had stated that the liquor store with its enormous profits helped the city financially, as well as solved the bootlegging problem.

"We need a sleep-off center for alcoholics," said a new Indian bureaucrat, thrust into his position because of the land claims act. "We show movies at the school to show the horrors of drinking.

"There is no case of child abuse due to drunkenness," he continued, but according to a village nurse there were four *known* cases.

"Those Natives!" white people would begin with a superior tone, and I would brace myself for the sermon about the amount of government money pouring into the communities. The land claims money was payment for land, not payment for services in the community.

"Agencies are set up but don't perform," said the Indian official. "They write reports. Politicians want our votes, but they don't want to listen to our needs. Once elected, they tell us they don't have the money to help us.

"What gripes me is people who come up from Washington, D.C. They spend two or three hours, make promises, but hardly any of the promises materialize. The bureaucrats hold on to their jobs, perpetuating the situation."

I sketched an Indian woman dressed like a gypsy, wearing a paisley blouse, her hair tied up in a violet scarf. Her heavy cotton stockings were rolled below her knees. She was making fry bread, the most common bread eaten on the Yukon.

She mixed about two cups of flour, two tablespoons of sugar, one teaspoon of baking powder, a dash of salt and one-half cup of water. Then she melted grease in a frying pan and fried the batter. She didn't measure a thing, but it tasted good with coffee.

When flour was introduced to Indians, they did not know how to use it, and the raw baking powder in the middle of the bread would continue to ferment in the eater's stomach. In those days some people chewed black plug tobacco and drank tea boiled hours and left stewing on the stove all night.

Their Kutchin ancestors had incised wood and bone and used porcupine quills, red ocher and berry juice to decorate clothing, but the students at the school where I taught an art class were unimaginative. Their teacher, Mrs. Peters, and I tried hard, but the students hid their drawings shyly, used rulers, shuffled their feet and painted in an inhibited way, evidently unaccustomed to the experience.

Two girls from the art class came to see me after school and, to my amazement, talked to me incessantly. I asked about the children's behavior in the classroom, and they replied, "They were scared of you. They get scared when they see new grownups." This was later verified by the teacher.

The girls told me about their summer experiences at fish camp. "Every day we get fish, we cut it or else the fish will spoil and the crows will eat their eyes. We cook the guts for the dogs and keep the fish eggs. When we smoke it, it keeps the flies away. You have to keep moving the fish so it won't get worms in it."

The other girl added, "We eat fish, we dry it, sell it, give it away and use it for dog food, or else we save it for winter."

The children, according to a school magazine of children's stories, believed in bushmen, who were supposed to be descended from outcast men who resorted to cannibalism in time of famine. I think the bushman symbolized their fear of being lost alone in the woods. "He sneaks around the bushes," wrote one little girl, "and steals little kids and cooks them for dinner. He's got a lot of hair all over him and he eats blueberries. He gets kids and ties them up and puts them in deep holes."

Some Indians believed in reincarnation. Generations of Christian in-doctrination, including hell-rousing preaching, had failed to affect this deep-rooted Kutchin belief that animals have souls; in mythical time they were of one kind, the caribou and the Kutchin. A pregnant woman who dreamt of a dead person when she felt the fetus move within her would watch for physical signs resembling the dead person when the child was born.

The anthropologist Richard Slobodkin, who lived among the Kutchin, wrote that an eighty-year-old woman appeared to be dying, but she was a tough old lady and lived another dozen years. When she was strong enough to speak, she told of her experience while dying: "I left my body lying in the tent and I rose up into the air . . . It was a bright, sunny day and I could see the whole camp. Smoke was rising, dog teams were going here and there, and I could see my great-grandson, Andrew, coming to my lodge with a load of good meat for me.

"Something was bothering me after all. I had to find a new mother, some woman who was going to have a baby. I thought of Rowena, Andrew's wife . . . but she was not going to have a baby . . . nobody in camp was. I could not be born again. I had to go back. I went down, through the wall of the tent and back into my body, and I woke up here, still sick."

The oldest Kutchin Indian lady I knew was Belle Luke from Fort Yukon, whom I used to visit at Careage, the convalescent home in Fairbanks. Her two husbands had been chiefs. No one knew her age exactly, but it was presumed to be over one hundred years. She used

to lie on her bed with her hair wrapped in a red bandanna, her mischievous eyes watching me. Only her front teeth were missing; her skin was stretched tight over high cheekbones. She called me "Grandchild." Friends brought her fish heads, moose, salmonberries and blueberries. She took only aspirin and Rolaids, refusing all other medicine. She looked healthy; it was good to be around her.

Last spring she felt lonely. "Grandchild," she said, "I'm dying." She sent a call out to all her children and grandchildren, friends and relatives, and when they were around her bed, she said, "I'm dying." She lay back to survey the brood of solicitous faces around her. "I'm dying," she repeated. The morning passed and it was time for lunch. She picked at it, then sat up, reached for a spoon of ice cream and lay back again. She took another sip of ice cream, then lay back again.

"I'm old. I lived a good life. I'm tired. I'm ready to die." Another sip of ice cream. "Doctors were good to me in Fort Yukon," she said slowly. "Doctors were good to me in Tanana Hospital, doctors were good to me in Anchorage, doctors are good to me here. But I don't need doctors no more. I'm dying."

Another sip of ice cream. At this point the head nurse, Donna Stevens, leaned over close to her ear. "Belle, I don't think you are dying."

"No?" she answered with a gleam in her eye.

"No. You just did ten situps for the ice cream and your appetite is good."

"Really," said Belle, and whispered back, "Well, don't tell anyone." Her relatives all went home, much to her disappointment.

Belle died two years later at Careage instead of at her own village. She died well, calling her loved ones around her once again and blessing them.

To be born Indian, to live as an Indian and to die as an Indian was important to her. Pride was respected and carried from birth to death, from the beginning of life to the end.

Had Belle been in her village, the women would have bathed her body, scrubbed her cabin and prepared quantities of food. The men would have gathered together to build a coffin and dig a grave in the frozen ground. All of the villagers would have packed into the church for the services, accompanying the coffin to the graveyard, singing hymns while the grave was filled with dirt. After that would come the great feast. The same custom was followed up and down the Yukon among Athabaskans no matter what their dialects or differences.

Hannah Solomon, who is from Fort Yukon, and I shared a love of berry picking. We would bend and pluck the cranberry rubies, inhaling their faint wild odor, kneeling in the soft sphagnum and mosses as if we were at some altar. To us, it was a needful act, totally engrossing our minds and bodies. On an autumn day we heard the rustlings of the aspen leaves and the call of the sandhill cranes miles beyond.

Hannah's grandmother probably stored lowbush cranberries in birch baskets, sewing a light lid on them, then burying them. The highbush cranberries, which had a more bitter taste, were mashed with bear or moose grease to keep from spoiling. Berries and grease were added to boiled salmon and stirred until the mixture foamed.

Hannah was a serious berry picker; her movements were quick and economical and her searching eye keen. Her bucket was always fuller than mine. She liked the black crowberries in the woods, difficult to find and bitter, while I passed them up for the easier cranberries. When I picked blueberries I stuffed handfuls into my mouth, seeking momentary pleasure, but Hannah's went into the bucket.

She was known for her beadwork, the pride of Kutchin women. Her designs were intricate floral and animal patterns sewn on tanned moose hide. Hannah now lived in Fairbanks and no longer needed to sew by candle or kerosene lamp.

Her husband, Paul, died in Fort Yukon at ninety-one, leaving Hannah, sixty great-grandchildren and seven great-great-grandchildren.

Agnes Peter, a strong-willed Kutchin woman of sixty-six, was a good friend. She and Charlie had sixteen children; ten died of tuberculosis. I loved painting her careworn face and solid body. She was ill now with arthritis and found it difficult to get around, living in Fairbanks to be near medical care, while Charlie lived at Fort Yukon.

Charlie played Kutchin dance music at weddings. He held his scarred and battered fiddle lovingly against his chin, his foot beating time as he played for me. His mother had bought him his first violin, or his "machine gun," as he called it, for fifteen dollars from a man on a ship. A schoolteacher gave him lessons for two years.

After Charlie was through trapping and the river was free of ice, he liked to go out in his canoe and play to the ducks. "The female muskrat likes the E string," he said. "They come out to listen to me."

"What do you do then?"

"I shoot them. Sometime there is no muskrat around, just a black crow listening to me."

"I like the outdoors. I don't like the drinking in Fort Yukon," said Charlie once. "I'd rather go hunt pintails and ground squirrel. Roast the duck on a stick. Find a nice place to sit in the woods. Make good hot tea."

"This violin cost me $378," he said another time, "and I been playing it for forty years. When I die, no one can take my place at Fort Yukon.

"When the Indians at Old Crow used to come to Fort Yukon, we learned the Virginia reel. They danced the double jig, with two women and two men. I learned to play 'The Cuckoo Waltz' from them." Charlie swears he plays "real Kutchin music," but it sounds to me like an Indian interpretation of Scottish jigs.

He told me stories about his grandfather: "Old William was out looking for birch to make snowshoes on the Chandalar River. He met a brown bear, who killed his dog. Old William had a short ax and he was fast and strong. He kept out of the bear's way, fighting hand-to-hand with him, and finally killed the bear with a blow to the head.

"When old William was young, the people were starving. No moose. No rabbit," continued Charlie. "They went to the lake and there was a big beaver house. Old William cut through the ice with a moose horn, then he dived under the ice, which was four feet thick. My grandfather saw the beaver all sitting around. He heard that the beaver never fight in their own house. He got string and tied the beaver feet. When he came out, people had a fire waiting. They pulled about six beaver out and everyone had a good meal. That's how Old William saved the people."

We talked about Shaynyaati, the last of the great chiefs of the Kutchins for half a century, who wore the red coat of the Hudson Bay Company hunter. He could kill caribou, it was said, when others could not even find their tracks. In return for furs, the company gave him tea, tobacco, flour, powder and guns. "He supported ten wives and all the widows and orphans," said Charlie. The minister had told him to have only one wife, but he was unwilling to do so and continued to support all of them. "He was a great hunter, killing a brown bear with his spear, stabbing him in the mouth."

Shaynyaati killed one of his wives around the time of the king salmon run. She was fooling around with another man, and when Shaynyaati came after her, she had a baby on her back and she was singing. Shaynyaati was packing a caribou and he just threw it off his shoulder like a little rabbit, threw down his gun, walked to her and said, "What are you singing?" He grabbed her and killed her with his knife.

Shaynyaati was buried at Circle, and for a long time the riverboat captains would blow their whistles when they passed his grave. Indian hunters traveling down the river shot into the air out of respect.

A one-room cabin was at the end of a long trail I walked. It was exposed to severe winds in winter, with a view of the flats and flying ravens. A young couple with two small children lived there. The mother's trusting expression, black hair and eyes endeared her to me. Her own mother, left with eleven children she could not feed, had given her away to another family. At twenty-five her body drooped and she had the listless look that I saw too often in the villages. Her lack of energy was probably due to afterbirth weariness and malnutrition.

She stooped over her washtubs sparse with water. (Ninety percent of the Fort Yukon people had no running water or plumbing.) Her small rented cabin, containing the necessary rudiments of living, was lined with cardboard walls, a common insulation and a fire hazard.

Her youngest child, only a few weeks old, slept in a modern crib. Her two-year-old sat trustingly on my lap and fell asleep in my arms. "Babies were wrapped in a blanket or shawl, then put in a birch-bark basket," wrote Laura Bettis in 1914. "They put in a squirrel's nest so it will be soft for us [the baby] to sit in. Then they tie us tightly into the basket and put a warm sack around our feet to keep us warm. When we cry they rattle the beads that are fixed to our blanket, and when we hear them we stop crying. They sing to us and then we stop."

When the young woman's husband, a carpenter, came home from work, her little one awoke, bounded off my lap and leaped into his arms. Father carried a great chunk of fresh moose meat someone had given him. This young couple was trying desperately to make it without relief handouts.

Poverty along the Yukon manifested itself through the cardboard-insulated walls and leaks in the roof during the spring thaw. For most at Fort Yukon, there was no electricity, except for that provided by one private company, and no running water. An outhouse or a five-gallon can sufficed in place of plumbing. Poverty was a widow chopping wood for the fire and going to the river to haul water from a hole in the ice at forty below zero. Poverty was a growing child eating only starchy

food and sleeping with three other wretched children on a single mattress on the cold floor.

I walked the length of the village back to the hotel in the dawn. The silver river was faint with misty light, contrasting with the somber mud flats and shabby cabins. Lemon birches glowed near the banks, and the wide-looping Yukon snaked through the gold hills as the sun set. Did the people rejoice at the beauty of the river and its reflected sunset, or was it just me, the visitor with a full belly?

CHAPTER 20

Circle City

*The dirty whites are flooding us from all
parts. A gasoline boat went up the Nowi
[Nowitna River] after the Indians with a
good load of hootch. Moral conditions were
distressing. Venereal diseases are becoming
an ordinary occurrence, a pretty safe mark
that the women are being corrupted . . . The
blessed martyr Ignatius had only ten
leopards, in the shape of soldiers, and I have
hundreds of ravening wolves, in the shape of
miners, saloon keepers, bums . . .*

FATHER JULES JETTÉ

IN 1893 Leroy McQuesten grub-
staked two Indians, Siroska and Pitka, to prospect in the Yukon. Their
rich strike brought miners to the spot that was subsequently named
Circle City.

The creeks' yield over the years amounted to over a million dollars. By 1896 Circle City had twenty-seven saloons, eight dance halls
and a Tivoli theater. The well-stocked library carried more than ten
thousand volumes. Stranded gold seekers such as Rex Beach, Jack
London and Joaquin Miller lived there and gathered material for their
books.

Circle, the largest log-cabin city in the world, was known as the
"Paris of the North." The dance halls charged one dollar for a three-
minute dance. Whiskey was watered to twice its volume and sold at fifty
cents a shot.

In those days a pall of smoke hovered over the Circle settlement in the winter, coming from a hundred red-hot sheet iron stoves, and in the summer from scores of moss smudge pots set out to deter the mosquitoes. Circle was a spectral place where the men exhausted themselves digging holes in permafrost and the prostitutes in vice. Most of the Circle prostitutes were a faded lot; they would not have come to this cold, remote spot had they made it in San Francisco or Seattle.

Most of the books of this period neglected to say how the Indians felt about all this; they were concerned with the white man's conquest for gold, and his gutsy preoccupation with the raw wilderness.

Hundreds of white men locked in during the long winters held "squaw dances." The violin notes spilling out of the dance hall enticed the Indian women in. The white men brought an excitement and novelty into their lives, flattering them with their attentions; and even though they could not speak the same language, dancing brought them in close contact. The miners danced bootless when the polkas were fast, becoming uncomfortably warmer, mingling the smell of rotten socks with whiskey fumes, cheap perfume and cigars.

The sale of liquor to the Indians was forbidden, but it went on in contempt of the law. At Rampart an Indian woman became so intoxicated by liquor given her by white men that in attempting to reach her home, a short distance from the scene of the debauch, she left her baby in a sled on the trail and it froze to death.

Wherever trappers and gold seekers gathered, they debauched the native women. All up and down the Yukon it was the same story. At Holy Cross, where the missions gave years of tender Christian instruction to the Indian girls, it proved to be a mixed blessing. By means of their superior education and cleanliness, the women attracted the attention of the more unscrupulous, lecherous white men, who tried to corrupt them.

Sam White, a bush pilot, told me that "just as soon as the girls came out of the missions, some men would drag those girls into their cabins and rape them. The men hungered for women. One month later and the woman would be knocked up by those bastards. The priests tried to prosecute the men, but I don't know if it did any good." Many of the Indian women desired white men and their material advantages, and some of the liaisons proved to be long-lasting, culminating in marriage.

I painted the silty water and a lone fisherman on the banks of the Yukon at Circle City. The landscape changed constantly. The sun, which had a moment before been shining on the distant blue-violet hills, geese flying overhead, now became overhung with dark clouds and storm. The flow of the river gave me a sense of impermanence; when I tried to capture it, it was gone.

Two Indian women walked down the road loaded with bucketsful of raspberries. A small Indian cemetery had gray fences with little carved knobs; the children's graves had spruces and fireweed growing on them. As I walked further down the bend, a huge black bear stood in the road facing me; then he turned and ran away while I stood there in amazement.

CHAPTER 21

Eagle

Long time ago the water flowed all over the world. There was one family and they made a big raft. They got all kinds of animals on the raft. There was no land but all water, and they wanted to make a world. The man of the family tied a rope around a beaver and sent him down to find the bottom, but the beaver didn't reach bottom; he got only halfway and drowned. The man then tied a string around a muskrat and sent him down; he reached bottom and got a little mud on his hands, but he drowned. The man took the mud out of the muskrat's hands into his palm and let it dry, then crumbled it to dust. This he blew out all over the waters, and it made the world.

Han legend of the creation of the world, collected by FERDINAND SCHMITTER, 1910

THE village of Eagle, near the Canadian border, is the last village on the Alaskan side of the Yukon River. When Schwatka saw Eagle in 1883, it had "six vintage aged cabins . . . the main street was so eroded that it was impossible for two men to pass unless one stepped into a cabin or down the riverbank. Racks of drying salmon. Hordes of half-starved old dogs roamed the village."

The people of Eagle are Han Indians, another branch of the Athabaskan family. *Han* means river as well as "People of the River." White men originally called Eagle "John's Village," after Chief John, who knew glitter from gold, for he trampled the glass trading beads offered to him into the ground. John's Village was eventually changed to Eagle because of the nesting bald eagles around the village.

I first met Sarah Malcolm of Eagle many years ago when she came to Fairbanks to visit her daughter. I've never worn anything as warm and comfortable around my ankles as her moose-hide beaded slippers trimmed with beaver.

She had sat in my living room talking about the winter in Eagle: "It was sixty degrees below for two weeks. No planes." Her eyebrows lifted in despair. "Nothing in the store; no oil for stove. Had to stay up all night to put wood in stove every three hours. Could hardly see out. I sewed these slippers in kerosene light."

I bustled around my kitchen making lunch while Sarah adjusted her scarf, a challis flower print, which she knotted over her forehead.

"I make fry bread. My kids like it. I make bone soup with onion, too," said Sarah, biting into her egg sandwich. "Roast beaver tastes just like chicken. My boys eat it with dill pickles or mustard."

Sarah's voice sounded muffled. Her brown oval face was somber, her mouth careful when she spoke. "Esau Benn was chief when I was a little girl," she said, admiring my china cup. I commented that I had painted his sister, Sarah Benn.

She continued with her own thoughts: "When I was twelve, people came from over the border in Canada to buy tea, rice and shells from us. They traded moose skins, fox, wolf, wolverine and lots of caribou skins and babiche; we traded for fish.

"They had a big dance, brought a guitar and violin with them. I watch, stand up on bench to see; I learned how to square dance." Sarah's eyes sparkled, and as if against her will, her mouth broke out into a low chuckle. "One time we danced a Red River jig and we taught them our dances."

We had another cup of tea and another slice of my carrot cake, then Sarah took out a birch-bark basket with little beads jingling along the edge. I bought the basket and a new pair of moccasins, as mine had completely worn out. Sarah walked to the door with a sliding motion, her eyes to the ground, carrying her purse and her shopping bag. "Clara, come to Eagle," she coaxed. "You would like it."

When I arrived at Eagle, situated on the silty brown Yukon, I was happy to see Sarah waiting for me. She lived in the Indian section of Eagle, separated by three miles and a long history of prejudice from the white section. In September, nestled against the bluffs, Eagle's small cabins with snow-covered roofs had lazy smoke pouring out the chimneys.

We went directly to Elva and Jim Scott's house, where Sarah was teaching a fur-sewing class. I joined the class, patching a new sole on Elva Scott's old moccasin. Sarah showed me how to twist the nylon thread using a strip of moose hide for reinforcement. She no longer tanned her own moose hides but purchased them from the Canadian Indian women.

I had met Cheryl Edwards, one of the girls in the sewing class, before. She was one of the "river people" who lived ten miles from the village. She had fleshed and tanned the beaver and wolf skins her husband had trapped and now, under Sarah's tutelage, was sewing them into a jacket.

Cheryl's grocery list was different from the bean-and-white-flour list the old-timers used to take into the woods. "We spent four hundred dollars on cracked wheat, dry corn, nuts, dried fruit, twenty pounds of wheat germ, oil and peanut butter. We get lots of lard from bear and moose, and I bake my own bread," said Cheryl. The Edwards grew their own vegetables and kept bees. "We shot four bears between us this year."

Other river couples lived a few miles from them. There was a road to Fairbanks, where they could purchase staples. The Indians tolerated them on their land, but were aware of every time that they shot a moose or a bear. Most Indian men were working for wages, but these young people chose the wilderness life style.

Elva Scott, who had organized the sewing class, was a village nurse, available at all hours to everyone. Jim Scott, a retired forester, had built their huge two-story log house, installing two airtight wood stoves and chopping all the wood needed for it. The Scotts were well prepared for winter with garden stuffs, berries, fish and wild game filling their larder and freezer.

Elva prepared a sumptuous lunch of smoked salmon strips, fresh salmon, homemade bread and fresh carrots. I contributed apples and some grapes I had brought, and we had coffee and cinnamon bread freshly baked in her wood kitchen range. The only lodge was closed for the winter, and Sarah's house was full; I was lucky that the Scotts invited me to stay with them.

Sarah talked about the old days. It was evident she was respected by this group of women, who appreciated her skills. She had been the teacher in a survival school for Indian children who had forgotten the old ways. Cheryl was eager to learn and she listened intently, since her life could someday depend on this knowledge.

"In old times, people don't know nothing about 'Sears,' they don't know nothing about 'sick.' Old people died from accident, sometimes from starvations," said Sarah. "No liquor or tobacco then."

"If someone broke an arm, he set and wrapped it in fresh birch bark, which dried hard like a cast." The people collected spruce pitch to use for infections; it drew soreness out of wounds. It was also boiled in water to make a drink for tuberculosis, and was chewed as gum. Spruce boughs were used for beds, the roots used for lashings and baskets.

Surgery in some tribes was the function of women because their fingers were considered more nimble. They operated successfully with flint knives. For snow blindness, women cut the swollen blood vessels with a beaver tooth or a bone needle. For certain stomach aches the end of babiche line was swallowed to make the sufferer vomit. Charcoal was drunk for bloated stomach and added to wound surfaces. Fish eggs and wild rhubarb were laxatives, and sweat houses were used for steaming and sweating out a sickness. A simple headache was relieved by putting the head in snow.

Sarah crossed her legs, which were covered in two pairs of woolen stockings and long caribou moccasins trimmed in beaver fur and bead-work of her own design. "If I had a cough, I chewed roots or spruce bark," she said as she lifted her cup and drank tea—Lipton's, not Labrador or Hudson's Bay tea, which was common.

"Women made fishnets and smoked king salmon day and night. They used to sell the fish for twenty-five cents," said Sarah scornfully. "Indians didn't have scales then."

Her eyes crinkled up, but her little nose was soberly straight. "My husband showed me how to build fire in cold weather. First I make kindling, shavings. 'Watch out for knife,' he tell me," she emphasized. " 'Use birch bark to make shavings.' I pile it like this, then get kindling on top, crisscross." She showed me, with her fingers crossed, how she laid the wood.

"If I got only one match, I get lots of dry wood. It's cold maybe, deep snow. If no dry wood, I dry wood under my arms. I put little paper in my pocket wherever I go, then I start fire."

Sarah knew how to construct babiche from caribou sinew to make snowshoes. She helped the men make a birch-bark canoe, showing them the best birch to cut, with few branches, sewing three long birch strips together with spruce root. "The men think it's easy till they try it. It's hard," laughed Sarah.

Sarah cooked spruce pitch with one teaspoon of oil, then smeared it over the bottom of the canoe with a big spoon. Then she put the canoe in the water while the pitch was still warm to see if it leaked.

I interrupted to ask her how big the canoe was.

"Big enough for one man and one caribou" was her prompt answer.

Horace Beiderman, whose white father and Indian mother used to run the store, was married to an Indian girl. The village seemed divided between white settlers and Indians, and Horace tried to bridge the gap. It was difficult for him, living in the white sector and representing the Indians at the Native conferences.

There were always a few white people like the Scotts fighting prejudice, but the reactionary element of rugged old pioneers—a residue of miners who had never struck it rich, trappers, misanthropes and religious fundamentalists—held sway.

"Indians don't come hat in hand anymore," said Jim Scott. "They used to chop holes in the ice for teachers' water, chop wood, be subservient to teachers, but the worm has turned. Things have changed since the land claims."

I asked Beiderman, who is a cat skinner and makes good wages, "Why don't they put in a co-op store like Beaver's?"

"We can't find anyone to run it," he said. He received a ten-thousand-dollar grant to fight alcoholism and used it to establish a community hall for games, pool and cards. "They could do a lot here, like put in a well, get electricity and better housing."

In the beginning of the twentieth century, thousands of gold seekers digging along every tributary of the Yukon swept into the Han territory. The city that sprang up offered wonders of civilization that were new to the Han.

During the gold strike, the town boasted an army post, a saloon, a dressmaker, a laundress, a lawyer, dog freighters and a piano player. General Billy Mitchell had built the telegraph lines through Eagle; Roald Amundsen, the explorer, had stopped there after a three-year voyage exploring the Northwest Passage; and Judge Wickersham had traveled there by dog team to administer justice. The town had built a jail and courthouse by taxing the saloons. Women of varying degrees of cultivation and virtue arrived.

By 1950 the Indian children were allowed to attend the school in Eagle City. Schoolteacher Ann Purdy, who married a native and adopted Indian orphans, was practically ostracized.

The first minister, Reverend James, and his wife, Anna, arrived with a piano, organ, church bell, washing machine, feather bed, china, silver, carpet, books and dried food, bringing an air of civility to the town. Hardened miners wept at the piano tunes, remembering home. The first Episcopalian services were held in the saloon, the floor covered with sawdust. The pulpit was a table covered with a wolf-skin robe.

Indians traveled from their village three miles away in sixty-below weather to attend church services. According to Mrs. Kirk, in the collection plate, which was a tin basin, they offered one caribou skin, two pairs of moccasins, one tablespoon, two plugs of tobacco, fifty-eight bunches of sulfur matches, and ten dollars and twenty-five cents.

Sarah was right—there would not have been room in her ten- by ten-foot green plywood house for me to sleep, as her middle-aged daughter was visiting her.

I placed the box of groceries that I had brought for Sarah on the table and then sat on the cot facing the large wood range while she sewed. "My husband worked on *The Yukon* for Captain Newcombe," she said. "My husband's brother and his family went hunting with us. We shared two big tents and stayed out till late winter. I put the baby in warm caribou-skin robe, wrapped him good. When my husband is out trapping, I light the kerosene lamp, build a good fire in stove. Sew moose-hide slippers, mitts, keep busy."

Sarah's son came to visit, and when I asked him why he was not married, he said, laughing, "Can't afford it." Which was probably the truth.

The Yukon was muddy in the summer, and water had to be fetched from a nearby spring or bought from the delivery man; rainwater was caught in a barrel under the roof. "I pay two dollars for fifteen gallons delivered," said Sarah, shaking her head.

"For water we chop ice four feet thick, chop, chop and chop. It gets tiresome," said Sarah's son.

I asked Sarah if she went "behind the blanket" when she was a young girl. She hung her head and then murmured, "I did." She looked at me a long time to see my reaction. "I didn't like it. My mother didn't want me to, but the other women did. I couldn't eat any fresh meat or berries. I stayed there for one month.

"I wanted to go to school, so I wrote a note to the teacher. He came and knocked at the door and said, 'Sarah, what are you doing there?' He took me back to school.

"Those old ladies were too old-fashioned," she said scornfully.

"Did you wear a hood?"

She said no, but that she was not supposed to look at the road or the river, or men; she was to stay in the house all the time.

"When I went to school I sat on the banks and watched the river and the trail," Sarah said, her eyes twinkling. "Nothing wrong happened to me."

At thirteen she was a rebel. I looked at her with her black kerchief rolled and tied over her forehead, her plump, sagging cheeks and her solid figure as she sat and beaded, and I saw a different Sarah. I realized she had fought the conventions of her day and that took courage, because girls who broke with tradition could have been punished by being compelled to stay in isolation another year, left behind in the camp or ridiculed. Yet I remembered Sarah yesterday waiting patiently at the store and the storekeeper ignoring her as he waited on other customers. Sarah was quiet in white people's company most of the time, yet when we were alone, she was outspoken.

"When my baby come, I try to be brave. I close my mouth, then the pain isn't so bad. I breathe only through the nose. I kneel, don't lay down."

I remembered when my first baby came. I told the doctor that I wanted to have it naturally, without anesthetic. He did not believe me, as few white women did that then. When the time came, I insisted, saying, "If the Indian women can have babies that way, why can't I?" And I did. Natural childbirth was not fashionable in 1947.

"The first time I saw a baby come," said Sarah, "I was scared, but not anymore. They call me to help this woman have baby. She was so scared, laying down and not moving. I told her to get up and walk, then I make her sit and kneel, and her husband help her to have the baby. After I wrap it in rabbit skins, I show her how to rub her sides and stomach to get the afterbirth."

The woman used to give birth away from camp, crouched over a shallow pit lined with dry grass. One woman prepared to receive the baby, while the other embraced her from the back. The afterbirth was buried and the navel cord bound into an amulet for the baby.

Babies were washed, greased and fed, not weaned for two or three years. After nursing a child, the mother gave him soup from boiled meat. Fat from the knee joint of a moose, impaled on a four-inch stick to keep the child from swallowing it, was used as a pacifier.

For toys the children were given whistles and rattles made from moose horn. When they were older, boys were given miniature bows and arrows and bullroarers. Indians make much of their young children, rarely punishing them or forcing them to act against their own wishes.

I had another friend in Eagle, Nancy Juneby, a linguist from the University of Alaska married to Jim Juneby, former chief of Eagle. Her gray-haired husband, in his late forties, answered my knock gruffly in a resonant voice: "Why the hell don't you come in?"

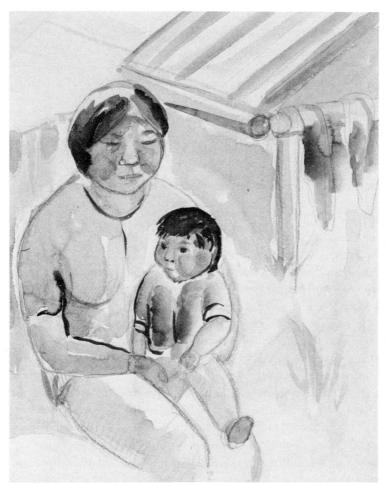

Nancy, a slim, graceful woman with curly black hair tied at the nape of her neck, was glad to see me. They had just returned from a wood-cutting trip. She and I had shared good times together at Sheldon Jackson College, she teaching Haida language and I art.

I explained to Nancy what Jim had said and we all laughed, which cleared the air. Maybe, I reasoned, the Indians just walked in without knocking.

Nancy invited me to dinner and set about cutting up moose meat. We made it a festive occasion. Jim opened a bottle of red wine, and we ate moose meat and onions on a bed of rice with crowberry jam. We made a toast in the light of the kerosene lamp to our mutual friend Fabian Carey, who had died recently; we drank to his exuberant spirit. Chief Juneby had swapped stories with him about trapping and wood lore. Juneby told how Fabian, many years ago, had invited him on the spur of the moment to fly in his plane to an old mining town for a drink at the bar.

Fabian had lived among Indians and trapped in the wilderness places where marten lived, traveling the rivers by boat and the trails by dog team, running on snowshoes. He had lived adventurously, surviving a plane crash and enduring months of isolation in his trappers' cabin.

After dinner we piled into Jim's truck to drive to the Scotts' place. The hardworking Scotts had a sense of proportion about life and its adventures. Jim was once mayor of Eagle, and Elva dispensed penicillin and other emergency medicines from her refrigerator. Seal skins covered their couch and chair, and Eskimo masks and Indian beadwork hung on the walls over their piano.

The Scotts told about a four-month trip to Russia, Sweden, Japan and Iceland, a month spent living among Laplanders. Jim said, "In all the world we traveled, we never saw as bad living conditions as right here in Eagle." There was no electricity, no running water or any place to dispose of garbage except in the Yukon. The town was in danger of flooding and no one could agree to move to a higher place. There was much talk, but conditions seemed to remain the same.

I thought of Sarah hauling every drop of water, sewing in the dark, her hand-to-mouth existence in that small house.

I later lay on the Scotts' couch listening to their cuckoo clock and watching the flicker of fire in the wood stove. New feathery flakes of snow were falling in the dark wintry night and the temperature was dropping. The wood fire went out every night and was built up again every morning.

In the morning I heard the grating of iron doors, the match striking and then the steady roar of a good fire. When I got out of bed, I inhaled perking coffee. Elva bustled around the kitchen range, stoking it with wood. Jim had gone down to the Yukon and caught two ling cod before breakfast.

Outside was a fairyland, with fresh snow on the tree limbs, pristine in its severity. The river still flowed, although slower, icing up with the coming of winter. Soon there would be a footpath across the river. The sun lit up the blue shadows and cast a fresh, airy look to everything. I filled my lungs deeply.

The picturesque log houses had jaunty whitecaps set on every crevice and fence. I walked about the town smiling at everyone, visiting the old church, the museum and Judge Wickersham's ancient courthouse as well as the deserted barracks where army men and horses were once housed. On a clear day you could look up the Yukon and see the hills of Canada.

At the schoolhouse I introduced Sarah as an artist of skin and beadwork, which was a new concept to the children. Evidently Sarah had never been invited by the schoolteachers.

The snow falling heavily all day turned the village into a thick painting, changing the log cabins into white princely chalets and the fields into feather frosting. Each footstep left deep, dark tracks, marring the immaculate perfection.

Sarah took me to visit Eliza, the oldest woman in Eagle, introducing me proudly and acting as translator. Eliza, a shrunken dark-skinned woman wearing a red kerchief, sat on her bed, her tiny feet poking out straight before her. She shared the cabin with her daughter, who was the cook at the school.

"Eliza is very old," Sarah translated, "maybe over a hundred." A remnant from nomadic days, Eliza used to carry her baby on her back while pulling the sled with her belongings, like aboriginal women. At night she made camp by staking bent willows, which she carried, then covering them with moose skins to make a tent shelter. She gathered firewood, building the fire in the center. The hole on top allowed the smoke out, but many of the old women, including Eliza, complained that it damaged their eyes, causing blindness.

All the anthropology books in the world could not convey to me the slightest impression that meeting Eliza did. In her body and presence was embodied the old life style of Athabaskan Indians; every wrinkle attested to this. Behind her eyes lay the old wisdoms, earned by hardship. She had the knowledge of walking snow trails with heavy burdens into unknown subarctic forests, knowing how to exist with "no grub," living off the land.

Eliza had dropped her babies alone, straining and squatting in the wilderness. She had worn a soft tanned strap of caribou as a brace below her stomach to support the additional weight of the baby. After the baby was delivered and the cord tied, she had wrapped the baby in soft moss and furs, secured it with a sash or baby-carrying strap and followed her people to the next encampment. She and other Indian women had a right to feel pride in their fearless attitude in giving birth alone.

Sarah had the highest respect for Eliza; it was shown in every word she spoke. I asked permission to sketch Eliza, feeling it a great privilege. As she sat there in the dim light, I asked her what she most desired from town. Sarah translated that she needed woolen stockings and undergarments, so I promised to send them.

The Indians are still fighting for the right to have their children taught by teachers who will not treat them as inferior beings. Sarah, a shareholder in Doyon, one Indian profit-making corporation, had a vote, but she and the other villagers seemed to be as poor and powerless as always.

The white section of Eagle seemed to debilitate the Indians, keeping them fermenting like yeast. The interaction was poor; there was little communication.

In the winter, snow was deep, winds unbearable, and temperatures sometimes dropped to almost eighty below zero. Indians and whites shared narrow village lives, confined by the cold that surrounded and imprisoned them. Some of the white people did not speak to each other for years over some infraction or stubbornness. Indians were spoken of in derogatory fashion. Whites remembered the percentage of Indian blood in each person.

Although the steamers no longer plied the Yukon near Eagle and dog teams no longer hauled the mail and supplies, the whites and the Indians of Eagle still lived three miles apart, with different life styles. The economy ebbed while the prejudices of the ingrown village prevailed.

CHAPTER 22

Potlatch

*The long line of twenty-six dog teams stretched
across the river, advancing a few hundred feet . . .
so as to make the approach more stately . . .
The Nenana Indians, lined up on the bank . . .
against the white of the snow and the gay red
and blue sashes of the men, and the feathered
headdresses of the women decked with ribbons
of all colors . . . Now and then a volley from the
rifles . . . The son of the chief is dressed in a black
colonial uniform . . . his cocked hat has a long
ostrich plume, and he handles the sword and
the megaphone . . . Chief Evan of Coschacket
and Chief Alexander of Tanana advance in
formation, charge towards each other on the
run, cheering . . . finally the visitors rush up
to the bank and dance among the crowd.*

REVEREND FREDERICK B. DRANE,
"The Potlatch in Nenana," 1916

TRUE to my promise, I returned to
the village of Minto to attend the potlatch given in honor of Chief Peter
John's son, Orion, and six other people. I had no sleeping bag with me,
and I did not know where I would sleep, for every house would be filled
with visitors and relatives.

Vi Hatfield, the wife of the local Assembly of God's minister and
the woman who came to the airport to pick up the mail, generously
invited me to sleep at their house. Such is Alaskan village hospitality;
I had never met her before.

The Hatfields lived in back of their church. Vi, who had Sioux and
'herokee blood, was a heavy woman with the proverbial heart of gold.

The Hatfields had come from the Ozarks to Alaska three years before because "Ralph had the call."

Their generosity extended to an Indian boy from Nicoli, who slept on one couch; a blanket used as a curtain separated his area from mine. The outhouse had a small stove, practical in cold temperatures; a pile of kindling and old magazines lay on the rude pole floor.

The preacher was quiet, in contrast to Vi, who loved to talk and cook. Their son Wade looked like an eighteen-year-old Gomer Pyle, right down to the accent.

In a house nearby, people were dancing in a circle, round and round, shoulders shaking, feet taping. When it was over, they came singing down the steps toward me. Rose David put her arms around me and hugged me warmly, whispering in my ear, "Clara, we're singing you the welcome song." She recalled a potlatch like this one over fifty years ago, when she was a little girl. "I'm Caribou," she said, meaning that her family line, the Caribou clan, was passed on to her children in matrilineal descent. "The children go by the mother," she said, sitting on the doorstep, tired from all the dancing. "I want my children to keep the tradition, to marry the opposite clan, not in the Caribou. They can marry in the Fish clan."

Chief Peter John addressed me. This was not to be an ordinary potlatch, he emphasized, "not just one of those Fourth of July potlatches. Six people will beat those sticks!"

"No picture taking," he later warned. I assured him I would not photograph the event. The villagers had refused to permit photographers from the University of Alaska to take pictures, and a reporter had been invited to leave when she had disregarded the rule.

Mrs. Peter John carried an armful of ducks to add to the broth simmering in a half-gallon drum over an open fire. Some young girls sat around cutting onions, potatoes, carrots and celery in small pieces for the soup while a woman nearby winnowed highbush cranberries, taking out twigs and leaves.

I left my box full of meat, candy and nuts, as I did not want to be fed without bringing my share of the food.

Richard Frank's wife was tending a moose hide in the smoke-house, folding it over a slowly burning rotten-wood fire. The hide had been tanned in the old way to give it a burnished brown shade, and she watched the embers closely so as not to burn the hide. Sometimes fermented moose brains or urine was used to tan skins.

Chief Peter John invited me to sit down, asking about my family.

I mentioned that I had not been able to attend my father's funeral in New York years ago.

Peter John looked at me searchingly. "You never got your grief out."

Then he asked me why women cry; he really wanted to know. I told him I cried to relieve tension, that it was natural for me to cry, and that contrary to Indian tradition, I did not hide my emotions. It was difficult for me to describe an emotion that I always took for granted to a man who did not believe in it. We ended the conversation in a strange way.

"You don't know me," he said.

"I feel as if I do," I replied.

Mathew and Dorothy Titus were Orion John's real parents, but they had given Orion to Peter John and his wife because the Johns had no son. Peter John and his whole family had saved and worked hard for several years to give this potlatch for Orion.

Janet Charlie, one of the girls also being honored at the potlatch, had been a religious girl. Mrs. Hatfield told me she had been engaged to a soldier stationed in Fairbanks. Although Janet had been brutally raped and mutilated, her mother prayed for the murderer's spirit, offering forgiveness to the madman. The other girl, Lu Jean Jimmie, had also been murdered, cut up with a chain saw, identified only by her engagement ring. The dogs found her dismembered body buried under the river ice.

State troopers had finally found the killer who had stalked Minto —a man who lived near Minto and who, since the age of six, had been in mental institutions. Arthur George Post admitted to the murders of the Minto girls. He had raped, beaten and burned a white girl who had escaped and identified him. Post, a thin, toothless madman who hated his mother, was eventually given a life sentence.

In the evening the community hall filled up gradually with older people who selected seats while their children ran about excitedly. White butcher paper was laid along the floor in front of the benches in a continuous roll. Tables were set up in the middle of the room and loaded with fourteen large cauldrons filled with boiled meat and other food. Two girls served buttered pilot bread, and then two men who had carried in giant kettles ladled hot duck soup into our bowls. The rich, gamy soup was full of rice, onions, potatoes and macaroni. Chunks of moose meat and whole bodies of ducks were then passed out. The dessert was green wild rhubarb and highbush cranberries boiled Indian style—with sugar and thickened with flour. It was impossible to eat it all; women saved much of it to take home.

After the food had been consumed and the place was cleaned up, the singing of mourning songs for each dead or living person honored at the potlatch began. The chief and his wife rose from the benches to sing Orion's song, circling around their daughter Garnet. She wore a two-feather headband, and as she beat the sticks, her hands were encased in moose-hide gloves trimmed with beaver. The chief moved stiffly, his arms hanging at his sides as he sang. Old Susy Charlie came over to sit on a chair in the center, where the women swayed around her, holding scarves and shuffling in their moccasins.

Young girls lined up to face the drummer, dancing the traditional welcome dance. One dance followed another. There were love songs and songs imitating birds and animals. An old lady leaning on her cane translated some of the Athabaskan for me. Virgil, Orion's half brother, danced with knees bent, waving his elbows, turning his head from side to side.

The women danced with dignified motions and holding scarves while the men made varied stronger motions within the circle of women. The women wore long fringed cloth or smoked moose hide which came down to their knees and which was embellished with beads and feathers. The men wore fringed moose-skin jackets, also beaded in elaborate designs. Young girls wore headbands decorated with porcupine quills; their moccasins were trimmed in beaver. Some of the single girls looked elegant, their shiny hair smoothed back over their ears, displaying long quill earrings. They held scarves of vibrant colors while they swayed rhythmically, their heads held proudly.

Mathew Titus' wife was honoring him because he had almost died last winter of an ulcerous lung and a weak heart. A faith healer who came to Minto had healed him, according to Vi Hatfield. She told me that when he returned to the Fairbanks doctor, only healed scar tissue was found. Mathew sang, a bit out of breath, near his son Virgil, whose face now streamed with sweat as he flapped his long arms.

Bessie Charlie and two other blind women in bright flowered kerchiefs clustered on the floor, moving their heads to the beat. An old woman in black danced with vigor, waving her arms strongly while everyone applauded.

Ninety-year-old Bessie, whom I knew from Fairbanks, danced in sneakers, a blue scarf knotted old style in front of her head. She was a marvel of strength, dancing faster than her daughter, displaying deep spiritual evolvement. She was the survivor of a village called Salchaket, and used to do a childbirth dance in which she leaned over a pole, squatting as she danced. The women also did a "washtub dance," performed with an up-and-down motion. One minister related that sometimes during the dance they became overcome with emotion and fatigue.

The drummer pounded his caribou-skin drum as hard as he could with his birch stick. Again food was passed around—dried smoked fish, doughnuts, cookies, cake, cigarettes, Coke and chewing gum. The mosquitoes also had their meal from the back of my neck and ankles. The rain had brought them out in full regalia; they took over the hall.

In 1915 Reverend Madara wrote: "We are trying to eradicate potlatches. At Nenana two of the men made a potlatch . . . the village feasted on 'white man's grub.'—boiled eggs, canned fruits, bread and jam . . . The other [man] had been out in the hills all that time, and he had no 'white man's grub,' but he had nine whole moose cooked up in every possible way, which he hauled in from his camp about ninety miles out in the hills."

A young boy came to sit next to me and asked if I was part Indian too. We both looked white, but what was inside our hearts only we knew. When he walked me home in the rain, the trees were dripping, the ditches were full of water and night was sky black. Every crater in the road held a small lake and a trembling moon.

I washed quickly and put out the light. The Nicoli boy was snoring behind the curtain, and the Hatfields were asleep in their room. None of the reasons they gave me for not attending the potlatch matched the unspoken reason. Was it against their fundamentalist religion? Did they feel it was a "pagan ceremony," as the Reverend Madara had? Reverend Hatfield had said, "I love Peter John, but he's doing his thing now. Everyone has his place." However, Vi made a brief appearance with me the next day.

Walter Titus and I sat in the morning sun drinking coffee. "The people are full of sorrow," he said. "The old ones remember the old days; people do not want the potlatch to end. In the old days it used to last for a month, not just a week. People danced all month; they never got tired. The men didn't lay around; they were too busy working. Things are different now."

There were over five hundred people here for the potlatch, the largest gathering for many years in the village. "We're close to a road. That's why," said Walter, filling my cup.

"There were three hundred people at Coschaket in 1914, when I was about five. We had lots of food and there was no store, just Native food. That old lady in black that danced last night was from Coschaket; she moved because they couldn't trap or fish anymore. Her husband died and the kids left.

"When my father was young we used to get together and play games. Young and old, it didn't make any difference, the old people used to keep up with the young. They were strong; nobody was sick then."

Across the street, people were singing, clustered around the central mourner. I heard a high, plaintive chant coming from an old woman sitting outdoors with her feet outstretched. Walter told me to go and say hello to her. "Tell her you were Louise's friend," he said. Walter's wife, Louise, had died a few years ago.

I walked over and touched her hand, for she was blind. She wanted to know if I was a Native, and I reluctantly said no. She seemed disappointed but continued to sing after I left. One of the Huslia women had sung a love song the night before; it was a haunting and beautiful melody, with Russian overtones.

The songs for the dead were sung only at the potlatch, but other songs handed down were sung over and over. A long time ago songs were considered gifts from the supernatural, revealed in visions. They were the essence of the individual's spiritual power.

The next evening the air was charged with electricity. Teenagers ran in and out, since no smoking was allowed in the hall. Everyone brought a plate, cup, spoon and knife (no forks). The men hauled large vats full of moose-head soup and then gave out huge chunks of boiled bear meat. I had eaten bear meat before but one piece of light gray meat with fat on it, which tasted delicious, was unknown to me. The old woman next to me did not know what it was either, but later I discovered it was boiled sheep meat, a delicacy.

Then came tender pike, full of bones, the finest baked king salmon, blueberries, oranges and candy washed down with strong sweetened tea.

After dinner the singers huddled protectively around the central mourning family. Peter John's back was expressive, hunched, stolid.

No announcement was made, but everyone applauded when a plain man with short gray hair simply sat down in a corner with the rest of the Tanacross people. It was Chief Isaac of Tanacross, arriving after midnight; his car had broken down at Tok, and when it was fixed he had to wait three more hours because of an overturned pipeline truck.

Dancers began to stomp, singing and moving at full speed. As soon as the drummer began a new song, one of the women would take it up and sing in a high-pitched voice. Robert Titus led the dancers with his six-foot stick, which was covered with fluttering crepe paper. Indians from each village sang their special songs until the people had

all memorized them: songs about virtue; mothers' songs of the children they had lost; songs of the moose hunt; songs of the squirrel ("He jump from tree to tree"); songs about the brothers or husbands lost in boating or hunting accidents.

There were many dances, some similar to square dances, with the women and men facing each other and dancing through the lines. Women applauded in their seats and shook, tapping their feet and swinging their scarves in the air. I kept time and shook like the women; I could not keep my feet or body still. Finally I jumped up and got into the circle, forgetting my shyness and the fact that I was taller than most of the women, my love of the dancing being stronger.

When I went out for a breath of air, a woman introduced herself as "Vernel, Ena and Peter Jimmie's daughter." She said, "My mother talked about you; you made her that dress that she used to dance in. My folks are dead now. This potlatch is for my father." I had forgotten about that dress, made about twenty years ago, when I first became acquainted with the Jimmies. I remembered Orion and Virgil as little boys dancing behind Peter Jimmie, copying his every movement.

Breakfasts of pancakes, bacon, eggs and coffee were served each morning, as well as liberal lunches; everything was supplied by the six families giving the potlatch.

After breakfast Sally Hudson, a friend from Fairbanks, and I walked down a muddy road lined with ripe rose hips. The sun blazed in blinding shapes through the spruce trunks, and spiders' webs glinted on the branches. Tassels of wild rhubarb waved in the wind, and unripe cranberry globes shone apple-green on the underside.

Sally, a stately woman married to a white man, reminisced about her grandmother, who had raised her. "We all begged her to take it easy, but she would not. At ninety she still walked to her trap line. 'I was raised this way, and if I stop, I'll die,' she told us. She was strong till the end.

"Doesn't it seem wonderful that all these songs from so long ago are still being sung and remembered, and not one of them was ever written down?" Sally said. "The people remember their hardships and history."

A relative of hers had composed a song after he had started out to Stevens Village. "A storm came up and he couldn't go home. He had a trap line and he couldn't get any fur; his family and relatives were hungry. While waiting in the storm, he wrote a song: 'What My People Going to Do?' " I had heard that song before. My neighbor Minnie, a

Koyukon woman, had sung it for me with so much feeling that I had cried.

Sally and I walked into Peter John's house as everyone was singing. Garnet, Orion's sister, wearing a dentalium headband, clapped the sticks, beating them as if she were beating pain itself. Opposite her stood Rose David's sister, Evelyn, hands curved to her heart, her feathered headdress shaking with emotion.

The chief and his wife stood stony-faced in the middle of a tight circle. As the chanting and keening went on, I wept openly. The old people moved their shoulders forward and backward, and I moved with them. The women sang shrilly and with great intensity, embracing after each song. One man, red-faced, was near the breaking point, but no tears flowed; it was his daughter who had been murdered. Another man left the room hurriedly; the women looked glassy-eyed, grief-stricken. I did not know how Mrs. John could bear it.

I sat near a sad-faced woman to hide my tears. Sally's jaw was clenched tight, the years of training apparent. Peter John sat in the rear with Chief Isaac, while Mrs. John disappeared into their bedroom. When I looked up again at Sally, one single tear had escaped, rolling down her rigid cheek.

Chief Isaac spoke in a voice hoarse with emotion and choked tears, for he had known much sorrow and death. I don't remember the exact words, but he expressed what we all felt about the Johns: "From my heart I speak to the great man who made this potlatch, and to all. We honor them in their suffering."

After the mourning songs were over, the mood changed to one of joy. An old man got up and, with a partner, did a double-motion dance. Their hands motioned in circles, first high and then lower, with a slight neck and head movement. Then they dropped their hands even lower, bending their knees. Sally leaned over and whispered, "That song is seventy-two years old."

The sad-faced lady near me with the rounded cheeks and braids and deep expressive eyes was Chief Isaac's wife, who had heart trouble and could not dance.

The rocking back and forth of the people reminded me of the old rabbis I had seen in prayer. In grief man is united with mankind, I thought. The joyous songs were a release from sorrow, toward the living. My eyes dried, I felt purified and drained; it had been a cleansing ritual. The chief had understood when I had spoken of my father's death. His face now looked new and washed as a baby's, all tensions gone. Without a break someone yelled, "Praise the Lord," and the old missionary songs began.

Wind roughly turned the yellow willow leaves over, revealing the gray undersides. The wood smelled young and fresh. The wind sang in the sky, up from the earth. From the trees a raven hovered. My life force flowed strongly from my heart to every living thing in a surge of joy.

When Peter John spoke on the last night, the teenagers' din blocked out his words. I was angry at their rudeness. The gist of his speech was that his grandfathers did the potlatch this way and it was a link with ancient times. "Traditions and customs passed on to every generation are important," he said. He hoped the potlatch spirit and atmosphere would unify everyone. Some of the rebellious teenagers did not want to keep the traditions; they had all been to white men's schools. Peter John was strict, objecting to their drinking habits, and they were angry because he would not let them have the hall for their rock-and-roll dances.

The chief reminded me of my father. I had asked my father, rebelling at his restrictions, "Wouldn't you rather be nice to me than always be critical and make me angry?"

"No," he had answered, "I'd rather you were angry at me and that I had told you to do the right thing." I had pondered that one for a long time as a teenager.

The Hatfields were eating lunch, but I was not hungry. I had stomach cramps, probably from the rich, oily duck soup. Or was it the porcupine meat? The children relished dried meat and fish, especially the porcupine. Those old ladies of eighty who danced night after night were raised on wild game. Vi told me that the duck soup may have contained muskrat, lynx and herbs. When I had asked what was in the soup, an old woman next to me had said, "Eat it. Eat it and don't ask what's in it."

Vi told me that the missionaries at Eagle were once given moose-head soup with an eyeball floating in it.

"What happened?" I asked.

"They ate it," she replied.

The final evening's dinner featured salmon, duck meat, moose-head soup, berries, tea and pilot bread. Weary children played tag while teenagers assembled into groups and pairs, furtively eying one another. Speeches were made by the older people, and I heard Orion's beautiful melody for the last time.

This time when Peter John stood up wearing his dentalium necklace, there were no rowdy teenagers, but absolute silence. He said, in effect, "Our Native culture was handed down from generation to generation. Every village has a different way to make a potlatch. That's the way it was handed down from our great-grandfathers. Too bad that we cannot understand each other [referring to the different dialects]. We are all Natives, we are all the same. We must love each other. With God's help we will see each other again."

In an answering speech Chief Isaac spoke hoarsely. I could hear only snatches of his oratory: "From my heart . . . be kind to one another . . . love strangers . . . Bible tells us to love one another."

Boxes full of presents were being brought out as the electricity failed and the hall, filled to capacity, was plunged into darkness. If it had been a crowd of five hundred white people and the lights had gone out, there would have been hooting, whistling and commotion, but here in silence people calmly took out flashlights. Finally someone got up, found a kerosene light and hung it from the middle of the ceiling. Seen in the dim light, this could have been a group of Athabaskans at a gathering many years ago, surrounded by piles of blankets and furs. After a long wait people quietly continued to bring out the rest of the gifts, not upset by lack of electricity; perhaps most of them had grown up without it. Eventually someone fixed the short.

Neil Charlie, wearing moose-hide jacket and gloves, gave out the first gift, a Hudson's Bay blanket and a rifle with a blue scarf tied to its trigger. I asked the Nenana man next to me why they were giving out gifts while wearing gloves. "That's the way it's done," he said.

Charlie Titus wore an old dentalium shoulder-to-hip knife sheath as he distributed his gifts. Peter John and his family distributed presents from six piles of goods as high as Mrs. John's waist. They gave gifts costing thousands of dollars, representing long cold hours on the trap lines, depleting all their savings and giving away their entire material wealth. Marten hats, afghans, patchwork quilts, moccasins, furs, snowshoes, gloves, rifles, coffeepots and many other articles were distributed by Chief Peter John's family.

The chief gave Orion's brother, Virgil, who was soberly dressed in his best clothes, a rifle, a blanket and Orion's moose-hide jacket. He then spoke kind words to him. The pile of blankets and gifts grew beside Richard Frank and others, and Walter Titus had a new pair of caribou leg moccasins, among other things.

Chief Isaac sprang up to say he wanted to explain to his people in their own language what was happening, inasmuch as their customs were different when they gave a potlatch.

Chief Isaac beat the drums while six Tanacross hunters jumped up to do the rousing traditional rifle dance, singing, stamping feet, posturing with their new rifles slung over their shoulders, the red-and-blue scarves zigzagging behind them.

Charlie Titus gave a rifle to the Nenana man who had found the body of Lu Jean, his daughter. A coffeepot was given out with the remark "You made my dad coffee." A suitcase was given to a woman with the remark "Now you can run away," at which everyone laughed. Enameled plates, snow shovels [also eliciting a laughing retort], goose pans, frying pans, fishing poles, skins of marten, and cash in ten- and twenty-dollar bills were given out. The Nenana man sitting next to me said, "That makes ten blankets I got." He was saving them for his potlatch.

The early missionaries were against the potlatch practice. In 1926 Reverend Wright had said, "As long as this system is continued, what is the chance for any advancement in the way of good homes and a progressive, providential community? . . . But so long as this custom is kept up, we will never be able to make the Indians a respectable and self-supporting people." (In 1920 in Canada, the Kwakuitl Indians had been jailed for giving potlatches. It was 1951 before the ban against the ritual was lifted.)

To the Indian the potlatch was an honorable ceremony, and in giving everything away, he gained prestige. He could give everything away and begin anew, a practice reminiscent of his grandfather, who walked out to hunt each day carrying all his possessions. A rich man who did not share his possessions was, to an Indian, a stingy man to be pitied.

Luke Titus, the Episcopal minister, came over to me during the dancing and asked, "Now do you understand Athabaskan life better?" I knew what he meant. At first I had felt like a spectator, but in sharing their grief and joy, I had "put myself in their moccasins." It was later when I was home that I realized I had been the only non-Indian at the last ceremonies in the chief's house. Someone had asked me again if I was an Indian; I thought it over and replied, "I'm not, but maybe I was in some former life." I identified with the Indian women. I thought Indian culture was a hard way of life.

A month later Walter Titus and I talked about the potlatch. "Clara," he said, "you gotta learn how to live in the woods, haul moose, drive dogs, walk in snowshoes."

My mind was elsewhere and I asked, "Don't Indians ever cry, Walter?"

"We were crying, but you couldn't see it, Clara. The tears were inside."

Bibliography

Adney, Tappan. Moose Hunting with the Tro-chu-tin. *Harper Monthly Magazine,* vol. 100, 1900.

———. The Indian Hunter of the Far Northwest, on the Trail to the Klondike. *Outing,* vol. 39, no. 6, 1902.

Allen, Henry T. *Report of an Expedition to the Copper, Tanana and Koyukuk Rivers in the Territory of Alaska in the Year 1885. Washington, D.C.: U.S. Government Printing Office, 1887.*

Amundsen, Roald. My Life as an Explorer. Garden City, New York: Doubleday, 1927.

Balikci, Asen. Family Organization of the Vunta Kutchin. *Arctic Anthropology,* vol. 1, no. 2, 1963.

Barbeau, C. Marius. Loucheux Myths. *Journal of American Folklore,* vol. 28, 1915.

Bettis, Laura. An Indian Girl's Alaskan Experience. *Alaskan Churchman,* vol. 8, no. 2, 1914.

Birket-Smith, Kaj, and Laguna, Frederica De. *The Eyak Indians of the Copper River Delta, Alaska.* Copenhagen: Levin and Munksgaard, 1938.

Boas, Franz. *The Tinneh Tribe of the Portland Inlet, the Ts'Ets'A'Ut.* Report of the 65th Meeting of the British Association for the Advancement of Science, 1895.

Brooks, Alfred Hulse. *Blazing Alaska's Trails.* Fairbanks: University of Alaska Press, 1953.

Cantwell, John C. *Report of the Operations of the U.S. Revenue Steamer*

Nunivak of the Yukon River Station, Alaska. 58 Cong., 2 sess., doc. no. 155. Washington, D.C.: U.S. Government Printing Office, 1904.

Carlo, Poldine. *Nulato: An Indian Life on the Yukon.* Fairbanks, 1978.

Chapman, John Wight. Athabascan Traditions from the Lower Yukon. *Journal of American Folklore,* vol. 16, 1903.

———. Ten'a Texts and Tales from Anvik, Alaska. *Publications of the American Ethnological Society,* vol. 6. Leyden, N.D.: E.J. Brill, 1914.

———. Tinneh Animism. *American Anthropologist,* vol. 23, no. 3, 1921.

———. *A Camp on the Yukon.* New York: The Idlewild Press, 1948.

Criminal Justice Center, *Alaskan Village Justice: An Exploratory Study.* Fairbanks: University of Alaska, February 1979.

Dall, William Healey. *The Yukon Territory.* London: Downey and Company, 1898.

———. *Alaska and Its Resources.* 1870. Reprint. New York: Arno Press, 1970.

Drane, Frederick B. The Potlatch at Nenana. *Alaskan Churchman,* vol. 10, no. 3, 1916.

Elder, Max Q., ed. *Alaska's Health: A Survey Report to the United States Department of the Interior.* Alaska Health Survey Team, University of Pittsburgh, Graduate School of Public Health, 1954.

Esmailka, Olivia. *Starvation, Nulato.* Alaska State Library Project, 1973.

Federal Field Committee for Development Planning in Alaska. *Alaska Natives and the Land.* Washington, D.C.: U.S. Government Printing Office, 1968.

Graham, Angus. Surgery with Flint. *Antiquity,* vol. 4, 1930.

Grauman, Melody. *Yukon Frontiers: Historic Resource Study of the Proposed Yukon Charley National River.* Fairbanks: University of Alaska and U.S. Park Service, 1977.

Gruening, Ernest. *The State of Alaska.* New York: Random House, 1954.

Helm, June. Bilaterality in the Socio-Territorial Organization of the Arctic Drainage Dené. *Ethnology,* vol. 4, no. 4, 1965.

———. The Dogrib Indians. *Hunters and Gatherers Today,* Marco Bicchiere, ed. New York: Holt, Rinehart & Winston, 1972.

———. The Hunting Tribes of Subarctic Canada. *North American Indians in Historical Perspective,* Eleanor Burke Leacock and Nancy Ostereich Lurie, eds. New York: Random House, 1971.

Hippler, Arthur E., and Wood, John R. *The Subarctic Athabascans: A Selected Annotated Bibliography.* Fairbanks: Institute of Social, Economic and Government Research, University of Alaska, 1974.

Hrdlicka, Ales. *The Ancient and Modern Inhabitants of the Yukon: Smithsonian Institution Exploration and Fieldwork in 1929.* Washington, D.C.: U.S. Government Printing Office, 1930.

Hulley, Clarence C. *Alaska, 1741–1953.* Portland, Ore: Binfords and Mort, 1953.

Jacobsen, Johan Adrian. *Alaskan Voyage, 1881–1883: An Expedition to the Northwest Coast of America. (Prepublication Notes.)* Reprint. Erna Gunter, trans. Chicago: University of Chicago Press, 1976.

Jenness, Diamond. *The Sekani Indians of British Columbia.* National Museum of Canada, Bulletin 84, Anthropological Series no. 20. Ottawa: Canada Department of Mines and Resources, 1937.

Jesuit Mission Records (Alaska): Holy Cross Mission File, 1898–1913. Microfilm. Oregon Provincial Archives, Crosby Library, Spokane.

Jetté, Pere Julius. *Alaska Jesuit Mission Records: Nulato Mission File, 1898–1920.* Microfilm. Oregon Provincial Archives, Crosby Library, Spokane.

———. On the Medicine-Man of the Ten'a. *Journal of the Royal Anthropological Institute of Great Britain and Ireland,* vol. 37, 1907.

———. On the Superstitions of the Ten'a Indians. *Anthropos,* vol. 6, 1911.

———. Riddles of the Ten'a Indians. *Anthropos,* vol. 8, 1913.

Johnston, Thomas F. Athabascan Indian Music in Alaska—*Vilitis,* vol. 38, no. 2, September 1979.

Kirk, Anna. *Pioneer Life in the Yukon.* Buffalo, N.Y.: Ben Franklin Printers, 1935.

Laguna, Frederica De. Indian masks from the Lower Yukon. *Anthropologist,* vol. 38, no. 4, 1936.

———. A Preliminary Sketch of the Eyak Indians. *Publications of the Philadelphia Anthropological Society,* vol. 1, 1937.

Loftus, Audrey. *According to Mama.* Fairbanks: St. Matthew's Episcopal Guild, 1956.

———. *According to Papa.* Fairbanks: St. Matthew's Episcopal Guild, 1957.

Loyens, William John. The Koyukon Feast for the Dead. *Arctic Anthropology,* vol. 2, no. 2, 1964.

———. *The Changing Culture of the Nulato Koyukon Indians.* Ph.D. Thesis, University of Wisconsin, 1966. (Ann Arbor, Mich.: University Microfilms, 1972.)

MacClellan, Catharine. Shamanistic Syncretism in Southern Yukon. *Transactions of the New York Academy of Sciences,* vol. 19, series 2. 1956.

McKennan, Robert A. *The Upper Tanana Indians.* Yale University Publications in Anthropology, no. 55. New Haven: Yale University Press, 1959.

———. The Chandalar Kutchin. *Arctic Institute of North America,* Technical Paper no. 17. Montreal: Arctic Institute of North America, 1965.

———. Athapaskan Groupings and Social Organization in Central Alaska. *Contributions to Anthropology: Band Societies,* National Museums of Canada Bulletin 228, Paper no. 4. Ottawa: National Museums of Canada, 1969.

MacNeish, June Helm. Leadership Among the Northeastern Athabascans. *Anthropologica,* vol. 2, 1956.

McQuesten, Leroy N. Ms., "Recollections of Leroy N. McQuesten of Life in the Yukon, 1871–1885," Yukon Order of Pioneers, Dawson City, Canada, 1952.

Madara, Guy. An Indian Potlatch. *Alaskan Churchman,* vol. 9, no. 4, 1915.

Mason, Michael H. *The Arctic Forests.* London: Hodder and Stoughton, 1924.

Mason, Otis Tufton. Cradles of the American Aborigines. *Annual Report of the Board of Regents of the Smithsonian Institute for the Year Ending June 30, 1887: Part 2.* Washington, D.C.: U. S. Government Printing Office, 1889.

Mathews, Richard. *The Yukon.* New York: Holt, Rinehart & Winston, 1968.

Michael, Henry N., ed. Lieutenant Zagoskin's Travels in Russian America, 1842–1844. *Anthropology of the North,* No. 7: *Translation from Russian Sources.* Toronto: Arctic Institute of North America, University of Toronto Press, 1967.

Morgan, Lael. *And the Land Provides: Alaska Natives in a Year of Transition.* New York: Doubleday, 1974.

Morice, Adrian G. The Western Denés—Their Manners and Customs. *Proceedings of the Canadian Institute,* 3rd series, vol. 7, 1890.

———. Dené Surgery. *Transactions of the Royal Canadian Institute,* vol. 7, 1901.

———. Denés. *Encyclopaedia of Religion and Ethics,* James Hastings, ed. New York: Charles Scribner's Sons, 1912.

Murray, Alexander Hunter. *Journal of the Yukon, 1847–48.* Canadian Archives publication no. 4, Ottawa.

Nelson, Richard K. *Hunters of the Northern Forests: Design for Survival among Alaskan Kutchin.* Chicago: University of Chicago Press, 1973.

Olson, Wallace M. Minto, Alaska: Cultural and Historical Influences on Group Identity. Ph.D. Thesis, University of Alaska, May 1968.

Osgood, Cornelius. Kutchin Tribal Distribution and Synonymy. *American Anthropologist,* vol. 36, no. 2, 1934.

———. *Ingalik Material Culture.* Yale University Publications in Anthropology, no. 22. New Haven: Yale University Press, 1940.

———. *Winter.* New York: W.W. Norton, 1953.

———. *Ingalik Social Culture.* Yale University Publications in Anthropology, no. 53. New Haven: Yale University Press, 1958.

———. *Ingalik Mental Culture.* Yale University Publications in Anthropology, no. 56. New Haven: Yale University Press, 1959.

———. *The Han Indians: A Compilation of Ethnographic and Historical Data on the Alaska-Yukon Boundary Area.* Yale University Publications in Anthropology, no. 74. New Haven: Yale University Press, 1971.

Oswalt, Wendell H. *This Land Was Theirs—A Study of the North American Indian.* New York: John Wiley and Sons, 1966.

Parsons, Elsie Clews, and Reed, T.B. Cries-for-Salmon, A Ten'a Woman. *American Indian Life,* Elsie Clews Parsons, ed. Lincoln: University of Nebraska Press, 1967.

Patty, Stanton. A Conference with Tanana Chiefs. *Alaska Journal,* vol. 1, no. 2, 1971.

Peter, Katherine. *Gineerinylyaa: A Book of Gwich'in Athabascan Poems.* Fairbanks: The Center for Northern Educational Research, University of Alaska, 1974.

Peters, Vivian. *Catholic Mission.* Alaska Library Project, April 1972.

Petoff, Ivan. *Report on the Population, Industries, and Resources of Alaska. United States Census Office, 10th Census, 1880.* Washington, D.C.: U.S. Government Printing Office, 1884.

Reed, Irving K. Frank Yasuda: Pioneer in the Chandalar. *Alaska Sportsman,* June 1963.

Renner, Louis L. Julius Jetté: Distinguished Scholar in Alaska. *Alaska Journal,* Autumn 1975.

Richardson, John. *Yukon River Exploring Expedition,* 1899.

Rothman, Stu. *The Untold Story of Hobo.* Ken Lavegne, 1975.

Schmitter, Ferdinand. Upper Yukon Native Customs and Folklore. 1910. Reprint. *Smithsonian Institute Miscellaneous Collection,* vol. 56, no. 4. Washington, D.C.: U.S. Government Printing Office, 1912.

Schneider, William. *Beaver, Alaska: Story of a Multi-Eskimo Community.* Ph.D. Thesis, Bryn Mawr College, Penn., 1976.

Schrader, Frank Charles. Preliminary Report on a Reconnaissance Along the Chandalar and Koyukuk Rivers, Alaska. *Department of the Interior, United States Geological Survey, 21st Annual Report, 1899–1900. Part II.* Washington, D.C.: U.S. Government Printing Office, 1900.

Schwatka, Frederick. *Summer in Alaska.* St. Louis: J.W. Henry, 1893.

———. *Along Alaska's Great River.* New York: George M. Hill Company, 1898.

Slobodin, Richard. Some Social Functions of Kutchin Anxiety. *American Anthropologist,* vol. 62, no. 1, 1960.

———. Kutchin Concepts of Reincarnation. *Western Canadian Journal of Anthropology, Special Issue: Athabascan Studies,* vol. 2, no. 1, 1970.

Steffanson, Vilhjalmur S. A Preliminary Report of an Ethnological

Investigation of the MacKenzie Delta. *Summary Report of the Geological Survey Branch of the Department of Mines, Canada, for the Calendar Year 1908. Sessional Paper No. 26.* Ottawa: C.H. Parmelle, 1909.

Stuck, Hudson. *Ten Thousand Miles with a Dog Sled.* New York: Charles Scribner's Sons, 1914.

————. *Voyages on the Yukon and Its Tributaries.* New York: Charles Scribner's Sons, 1925.

Sullivan, Robert J. *The Ten'a Food Quest.* The Catholic University of America, The Catholic University of America Press, Anthropological Series No. 11, Ph.D. Thesis. Washington, D.C.: The Catholic University of America Press, 1942.

Theata magazine, University of Alaska, vol. 1, 1973; vol. II, 1974.

U.S. Senate, *Alaska Native Land Claims Hearings Before the Committee on Interior Insular Affairs.* 90 Cong. February 8, 9, 10, 1968. Washington, D.C.: U.S. Government Printing Office, 1968.

Van Stone, James W. *The Changing Culture of the Snowdrift Chipewyan.* National Museum of Canada, Bulletin no. 209, Anthropological Series no. 74, Ottawa: Queen's Printer, 1965.

————. *Athapaskan Adaptations: Hunters and Fishermen of the Subarctic Forests.* Chicago: Aldine, 1974.

————. ed. Russian Exploration in the Interior of Alaska: An Extract from the Journal of Andrei Glazunov. *Pacific Northwest Quarterly,* vol. 50, no. 2, April 1959.

Vaudrin, Bill. Tanana Tales from Alaska. *The Civilization of the American Indian.* Norman: University of Oklahoma Press, 1969.

Whymper, Frederick. Russian America—Alaska: The Natives of the Youkon River and Adjacent Country (1868). *Transactions of the Ethnological Society of London,* vol. VII, London: John Murray, 1869.

————. *Travel and Adventure in the Territory of Alaska.* 1868. Reprint. (Ann Arbor, Mich: University Microfilms, 1969.)

Wickersham, James. Old Yukon Tales—Trails—and Trials. Washington, D.C.: Washington Law Book Company, 1938.

Wright, Arthur R. The Potlatch—What Is It? *Alaskan Churchman,* vol. 20, no. 1, 1926.

About the Author

CLAIRE FEJES was born in New York City. She studied painting and sculpture at the Art Students League. She has had eight one-woman museums shows: at the Frye Art Museum in Seattle; the Charles Bower Museum in Santa Barbara, California; the Norfolk Museum in Virginia; the Alaska State Museum in Juneau; and the Anchorage Historical and Fine Arts Museum. Her works are in the permanent collections of the West Point Museum in New York and the Williamstown Museum in Massachusetts. Her previous books are *People of the Noatak* and *Enūk My Son.* She lives in Fairbanks, Alaska, with her husband, Joe.